I0801849

Toward Infrastructure Improvement

An Agenda for Research

COMMITTEE FOR AN INFRASTRUCTURE TECHNOLOGY RESEARCH AGENDA

BUILDING RESEARCH BOARD

GEOTECHNICAL BOARD

COMMISSION ON ENGINEERING AND TECHNICAL SYSTEMS

NATIONAL RESEARCH COUNCIL

James P. Gould
Andrew C. Lemer
Editors

NATIONAL ACADEMY PRESS
WASHINGTON, D.C. 1994

NOTICE: The project that is the subject of this report was approved by the Governing Board of the National Research Council, whose members are drawn from the councils of the National Academy of Sciences, the National Academy of Engineering, and the Institute of Medicine. The members of the committee responsible for the report were chosen for their special competences and with regard for appropriate balance.

This report has been reviewed by a group other than the authors according to procedures approved by a Report Review Committee consisting of members of the National Academy of Sciences, the National Academy of Engineering, and the Institute of Medicine.

Funding for the project was provided through the following agreement between the indicated federal agency and the National Academy of Sciences: National Science Foundation Grant No. MSS-9116411, under master agreement 8618642.

Library of Congress Catalog Card Number: 94-67335
International Standard Book Number: 0-309-05144-4

Additional copies of this report are available from:
National Academy Press
2101 Constitution Avenue, NW
Box 285
Washington, D.C. 20055
800-624-6242 or 202-334-3313 (in the Washington Metropolitan Area)

Printed in the United States of America

COMMITTEE FOR AN INFRASTRUCTURE TECHNOLOGY RESEARCH AGENDA

Chairman

JAMES P. GOULD, Partner, Mueser Rutledge Consulting Engineers, New York, New York

Members

EDWARD COHEN, Managing Partner, Ammann and Whitney, Consulting Engineers, New York, New York
THOMAS J. EGGUM, City Engineer, Department of Public Works, City of St. Paul, Minnesota
EZRA D. EHRENKRANTZ, Chair, Architecture and Building Science, School of Architecture, New Jersey Institute of Technology, Newark
CARL MONISMITH, The Robert Horonjeff Professor of Civil Engineering, University of California at Berkeley, Department of Civil Engineering
ROBERT S. O'NEIL, President, De Leuw, Cather & Company; President, Parsons Transportation Group, Washington, D.C.
THOMAS D. O'ROURKE, Professor of Civil Engineering, Cornell University, Ithaca, New York
JOSEPH C. PERKOWSKI, Manager, Advanced Civil Systems, R&D Bechtel National, Inc., San Francisco, California
JOHN RAMAGE, Vice President, CH2M Hill, Inc., Milwaukee, Wisconsin
SARAH SLAUGHTER, Assistant Professor, Civil Engineering, Lehigh University, Center for Advanced Technology for Large Structural Systems, Bethlehem, Pennsylvania
JOEL A. TARR, Richard S. Caliguiri Professor of Urban and Environmental History and Policy, Carnegie Mellon University, Pittsburgh, Pennsylvania

Liaison Members

KEN P. CHONG, Director, Structural Systems and Construction Processes Program, National Science Foundation, Arlington, Virginia
JOHN B. SCALZI, Program Director for Structures and Building Systems, National Science Foundation, Arlington, Virginia
MEHMET T. TUMAY, Director, Geomechanics Program, Directorate for Engineering, National Science Foundation, Arlington, Virginia

National Research Council Liaison Representatives

NANCY RUTLEDGE CONNERY, Consultant, Public Works Infrastructure, Woolwich, Maine
ALBERT A. GRANT, Chairman, Committee on Infrastructure Consultant, Potomac, Maryland
RITA B. LEAHY, Strategic Highway Research Program; Visiting Assistant Professor, Department of Civil Engineering, Oregon State University, Corvallis

Staff

MAHADEVAN MANI, Director, Division of Infrastructure, Energy, and Environmental Engineering
ANDREW C. LEMER, Director, Building Research Board (1988–1993)
PETER H. SMEALLIE, Staff Officer
PATRICIA M. WHOLEY, Staff Associate
MARY McCORMACK, Project Assistant

CONTENTS

List of Illustrations

"INFRASTRUCTURE BLUES"

Replacing a 48" water main along Hudson Street in Greenwich Village, Manhattan, created havoc with the neighborhood. Begun in January 1992, to be completed in June 1994, it was halted periodically by rejection of the new pipe, teamster strikes, conflicting utilities, threat of contractor default, and holiday shutdowns and may be completed before June 1995. Developments in trenchless technology—for installation, renovation, and replacement of underground utility systems without open cut construction—has been rapid and extensive. The benefits of this technology in urban applications include reduced disruption of street traffic and adjacent businesses, longer service life of street pavement, improved safety for construction personnel, and ground movement and vibration hazards to nearby structures.
(Photo courtesy of The New York Times)

EXECUTIVE SUMMARY

Millions of Americans rely on the services of the nation's infrastructure, arguably the most extensive system in the history of mankind. Most of the time and in most places, the roads, water supplies, waste-disposal facilities, and other elements of infrastructure serve efficiently and reliably the wide range of economic and social activities comprising our daily lives, and few people really notice that the system is there. But sometimes a ruptured water main, street repairs, or the destruction from a major storm or earthquake provides unfortunate reminders of the infrastructure's significance.

The product of centuries of technological development and decades of construction, maintenance, and management, the system has developed for the most part as separate and distinct power plants, roads, pipelines, and waste repositories, built and operated by a myriad of government agencies, independent authorities, and private corporations. Decisions made in earlier times—when populations were smaller, land was less intensively used, and we understood less about our environment—leave us with facilities that are aging and often incapable of serving today's demands, some of them urgent. At the same time, extraordinary advances in electronics, biotechnology, materials, and other scientific and technical fields offer unprecedented opportunities for enhancing the system's performance. Decisions made today foreclose opportunities when we lack ability to project consequences.

Our infrastructure can be improved, and research is a wellspring for improvement. The National Science Foundation (NSF), created to increase the nation's base of scientific and engineering knowledge and strengthen its ability to conduct research in all areas of science and engineering, has been working to define the scope and extent of a program in Civil Infrastructure Systems (CIS). The NSF asked the National Research Council's (NRC) Building Research Board (BRB), in cooperation with the Geotechnical Board (GEOB), to undertake a study to provide advice on an infrastructure research agenda (Chapter 1). This report documents the work and recommendations of the committee appointed to undertake that study.

INFRASTRUCTURE AS A SYSTEM

The basic premise that infrastructure is an integrated system was adopted early in the study, and led the committee to look beyond its initial scope to a broader range of research needs and opportunities. The artificial disciplinary and institutional divisions among infrastructure modes and professions are largely historical artifacts that impose barriers to development and adoption of new technology. The NSF can make a great contribution to progress in enhancing the nation's infrastructure by continuing to adopt this broad view and thereby fostering a truly interdisciplinary approach to infrastructure research.

Infrastructure comprises both private- and public-sector elements, and current trends toward privatization of some modes while others are shifting toward greater government involvement make it difficult to state a sharp definition of "public." Nevertheless, "public" conveys meanings related to service to the public, public ownership or operation, and public-sector economics that can be used to guide—but not to constrain tightly—the scope of this infrastructure research agenda.

Efforts to improve public infrastructure are most frequently targeted at immediate problems, but the medium-term future—ten to twenty years hence—offers opportunities for greater influence in the long physical life of infrastructure facilities and technologies. However, rapid major change in existing networks and patterns of urban development are unlikely to occur within the time frame of a realistic research agenda. This study therefore focused on a search for infrastructure technologies that (1) are suited to incorporation within or overlay on current systems, without requiring substantial destruction of existing urban fabric, (2) permit alternative future urban development and are unlikely to damage the viability of existing urban areas, and (3) are likely to have value cutting across the distinct functional modes of infrastructure.

INFRASTRUCTURE RESEARCH AND THE NSF'S ROLE

Information on the overall level and scope of U.S. spending on infrastructure research, development, and technology adaptation activities is not well developed. Spending occurs in both public and private sectors, and in uncoordinated individual municipalities and commercial enterprises as well as large government or corporate programs. Study estimates place the total annual research and development (R&D) spending on infrastructure-related technology in the United States at approximately $2.2 billion, much of it in areas of technology generally associated with the civil engineering profession. This spending supports research at government laboratories, universities, quasi-governmental laboratories, and private research organizations; and much of it is directed at investigation of specific problems encountered in practice (Chapter 2).

The federal government is the principal source of infrastructure research spending overall, but the level of effort varies substantially among infrastructure's principal functional modes. At the one extreme, highway research has long been reliably supported by budget allocations from federal and state gasoline tax revenues and is conducted in many government laboratories (federal and state), universities, and many private companies. At the other extreme, institutional buildings receive very little explicit attention as infrastructure, and building research on the whole receives very limited funding.

Some private sector spending on infrastructure research does occur, most notably through industry groups such as the Gas Research Institute (GRI) and the Electric Power Research Institute (EPRI) and, on smaller scales, the research foundations established by professional and trade groups such as the American Society of Civil Engineers (ASCE), American Public Works Association (APWA), and American Water Works Association (AWWA).

The NSF provides a relatively small share of the total national spending on infrastructure research, concentrated on the nation's colleges and universities. However, the NSF is unique in its support of the knowledge base of engineering and science intended to foster technological innovation throughout the nation's economy. The NSF's independence and freedom from association with any particular infrastructure mode or interest group allows the agency's spending to be directed in a neutral and nonproprietary manner that offers opportunity for infrastructure innovation. This innovation occurs when industry or government apply the results of research.

NICHE OPPORTUNITIES

In view of the nation's needs and the NSF's role as a research sponsor, the committee developed a research agenda focused in seven broad cross-cutting niches (Chapters 3 through 9). These niches are essentially clusters of common science and technology issues that researchers may study both as areas for general expansion of scientific knowledge (e.g., in mathematics, economics, materials sciences, computer sciences) and as problems to be solved for individual infrastructure modes:

- systems life-cycle management, including plant or network operations, asset deployment, maintenance practices, system performance assessment and control, management, renewal decisions, quality of life and environmental management, throughout all stages of the life cycle from initial materials production to final facility demolition and waste disposal (Chapter 3);
- analysis and decision tools, for planning and design, needs assessment, dealing with capacity issues (Chapter 4);
- information management, including data collection, storage, assessment, and retrieval in forms that support decision making (Chapter 5);
- condition assessment and monitoring technology, for facilities and service performance (e.g., flow metering, effluent content) (Chapter 6);
- the science of materials performance and deterioration, including mechanical and chemical behavior, changes with time and use (Chapter 7);
- construction equipment and procedures, including construction management methodology (Chapter 8); and
- technology management, such as selection of treatment process or transport mode, bases for decision making, and environmental or social consequences (Chapter 9).

Within each of these seven niche areas are many researchable topics. The committee selected example topic areas (see Table 1) that seem highly likely to offer solid payoffs (i.e., research results that can be put into practice to yield identifiable benefits). However, many other worthy topics might be proposed by infrastructure researchers. Research is an exploration that often leads in unforeseen directions. The NSF should continue to support research less directly targeted on specific immediate applications.

RESEARCH LEADING TO INFRASTRUCTURE IMPROVEMENT

The topics and typical research questions comprising this agenda are intended as guidance to the NSF and the research community, but should not constrain the range or focus of specific programs and proposals. Allowance should always be made for new ideas and serendipitous results. Monitoring and evaluation of results coming from ongoing research should be a cornerstone of the NSF infrastructure research program (Chapter 10).

In the past, the NSF's spending has been allocated and administered primarily along disciplinary lines, matched to the structure of academic institutions that are the NSF's primary grant recipients. However, from time to time, special programs have encouraged collaboration across academic disciplinary boundaries or addressed needs not easily placed within traditional organizational structures, such as research centers focused on earthquake engineering, portland cement technology, and large-scale structures.

Both centers of concentrated effort and the work of individual researchers can contribute to achieving a high likelihood of payoffs from infrastructure research. Infrastructure is largely a local matter, and diversity of effort is needed to match the diversity of local conditions and demands that infrastructure must serve.

However, partnerships of researchers and research users can provide the crucial linkage for moving research results into practice. Such partnerships may involve either individual researchers or centers of focused research efforts.

Cross-cutting infrastructure research may be based at academic institutions, but could as well draw on the resources of government laboratories now being directed toward commercial activity and civilian concerns. NSF-funded programs could augment activities established under other government programs. Municipal and state governments should be partners in this research as well, to assure that research results can be tested in practice.

Regardless of the institutional setting within which the NSF-sponsored infrastructure research is undertaken, a single, unified program announcement, spanning all areas of infrastructure research, will best convey the cross-cutting philosophy embodied in the committee's agenda.

Investment in infrastructure research is well justified by valuable benefits to be gained: greater durability and enhanced performance for the physical infrastructure, the training of a new generation of infrastructure professionals, environmental protection, greater economic productivity, and improved quality of life for everyone who uses the infrastructure.

Innovation and infrastructure improvement are achieved through research only if results are put into practice. Research partnerships, involving municipal government, the private sector, and academic researchers in the quest for cross-cutting new knowledge and technology, will foster applications and build confidence in the methods and value of research. The essence of this value is reflected in words used by President John F. Kennedy and his brothers: "Some men see things as they are and say 'Why?' I dream of things that never were, and say, 'Why not?'" Infrastructure research should be an effort to dream of improvements and find ways to make them happen.

TABLE 1 Infrastructure Research Niches and Suggested Topic Areas

SYSTEMS LIFE-CYCLE MANAGEMENT (Chapter 3)

INFRASTRUCTURE DEMAND AND SERVICE LIFE MANAGEMENT

- Issues of Public Goods Demand, Prices, and Costs
- Managing Derived Demand
- Infrastructure as a Life-Cycle Production Process
- Assessing Consequences of Materials Innovation

TOTAL SYSTEM INVENTORY, MONITORING, AND MANAGEMENT

- Analytical Inventories of Infrastructure Systems
- Statistical Analyses and Benchmarking of Infrastructure
- Deviations-Detection Systems for Public Health and Safety
- Quicker Response Infrastructure Management
- Infrastructure Junction Points and Common-Use Corridors
- Private and Public Interface in Infrastructure

STANDARDS, REGULATIONS, AND OTHER EXTERNAL INFLUENCES

ANALYSIS AND DECISION TOOLS (Chapter 4)

SYSTEMS MODELS

- Ex Post Analysis of Planning and Design Methods
- Demand/Capacity Analysis

FASTER INTEGRATION OF NEW TECHNOLOGY INTO DESIGN PRACTICE

ANTICIPATING CONSEQUENCES OF CATASTROPHIC EVENTS

- Construction Effects on Lifeline Systems
- Emergency Infrastructure Operations Procedures

INFORMATION MANAGEMENT (Chapter 5)

ADVANCED DATA ACQUISITION AND MANAGEMENT METHODS

- Remote Satellite Imagery
- Improved Use of Supervisory Control and Data Acquisition Technology (SCADA)

NETWORK ANALYSIS METHODS

- Aggregation and Disaggregation Methods
- Intermodal Interactions

EDUCATION FOR INFRASTRUCTURE MANAGEMENT

- Using Information Highways
- Uses of Multi-Media

CONDITION ASSESSMENT AND MONITORING TECHNOLOGY (Chapter 6)

NONDISRUPTIVE, NONDESTRUCTIVE, CONDITION-MONITORING TECHNIQUES

- Structural Assessment
- Site Characterization

SYSTEM-WIDE CONDITION ASSESSMENT

ENVIRONMENTAL FACTORS AND MANAGEMENT OF RESIDUALS

- Chemical Grouting
- Management of Infrastructure Waste and Residuals

TABLE 1 (Continued)

SCIENCE OF MATERIALS PERFORMANCE AND DETERIORATION (Chapter 7)

HIGH-PERFORMANCE MATERIALS

- Polymers
- Geosynthetics
- Other High-Performance Material Applications

CHARACTERIZATION OF DAMAGE, DETERIORATION, AND AGING

- Limit States and Failure Criteria
- Time-Dependent Deformation and Strength
- Cost-Effectiveness Assessment

CONSTRUCTION EQUIPMENT AND PROCEDURES (Chapter 8)

HIGH-PERFORMANCE CONSTRUCTION TECHNIQUES

- Improved Information Exchange
- Off-Site Pre-Fabrication
- Resource Scheduling

CONSTRUCTION WASTE DISPOSAL

- Dredge Spoil
- Characterization and Assessment of Contaminated Sites
- Dry Construction Waste

UNDERGROUND CONSTRUCTION

- Automated Tunneling
- Trenchless Technology
- Hazards Mitigation
- Construction Effects on Adjacent Facilities

CONSTRUCTION SAFETY

REHABILITATION AND RETROFIT

- System Isolation
- Access to Degraded Segments

DECOMMISSIONING

- Temporary Facilities
- Network Devolution

PROCUREMENT AND MANAGEMENT PRACTICES

- Contracting Practices
- Project Management Tools

TECHNOLOGY MANAGEMENT (Chapter 9)

ACHIEVING HIGH PERFORMANCE

- Defining and Measuring Performance
- Incorporating "Externalities"
- Emergency Procedures

TECHNOLOGY ADAPTATION TO INFRASTRUCTURE

- Technology Compatibility Assessment
- Analysis of Technology Markets

INSTITUTIONAL OBSTACLES TO INNOVATION

- Criteria and Standards
- Impact of Procurement Methods
- Performance/Cost Trade-Offs Under Uncertainty

RESEARCH-TO-INNOVATION PROCESS

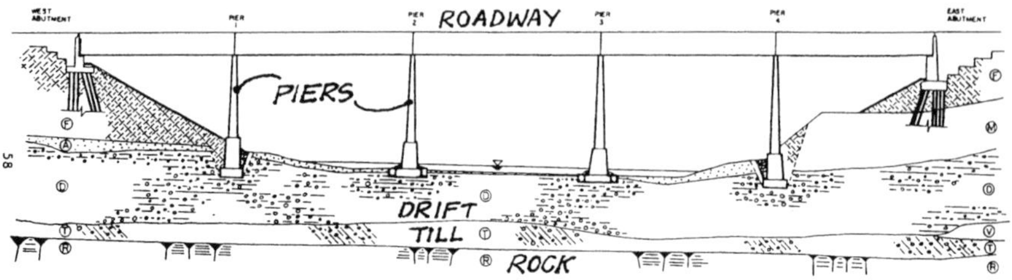

FAILURE OF SCHOHARIE CREEK BRIDGE, NEW YORK

Schoharie Creek Bridge failed in 1987 due to undermining of the shallow foundations of its piers by a near-record spring flood. Over the bridge's 33-year life, the originally meager rip rap protection of the piers was gradually dispersed. No effective periodic assessment was made to warn of the deterioration of the rip rap, on the basis of which remedial measures could have been taken. Current condition assessments, using both visual and mechanical nondestructive evaluation methods, are meant to provide data for deciding on effective maintenance, rehabilitation, and replacement actions. Research on assessment methods could enhance timelines and availability of information for decision making.

1

INTRODUCTION

Millions of Americans arise each morning expecting that they will be able to drink clean water from their bathroom taps, use electric power to read their newspapers or receive telecast news, and travel from their homes by transit or road to jobs and schools. As the day progresses, millions will use telephones, travel long distances by air and rail, and dispose of massive amounts of waste, all in the course of their daily activities.

Most of the time and in most places, the nation's roads, water supplies, waste disposal, and other infrastructure serve efficiently and reliably the wide range of economic and social activities comprising our daily lives. So effective is this technological system that few people especially note it. But sometimes a ruptured water main floods streets, transit tunnels, and downtown businesses, or street repairs break communications lines needed for airport operations, and we are reminded in most unfavorable terms of infrastructure's significance.[1]

The United States is served by what is arguably the most extensive infrastructure in history. The product of centuries of technological development and decades of construction, maintenance, and management, this system of roads and sewers, pipelines, and power plants is a valuable asset that contributes substantially to the quality of our lives.

This asset[2] has developed, for the most part, as separate and distinct generating plants, highways, waste repositories, and other facilities built and operated by a myriad of government agencies, independent authorities, and private corporations. Decisions made in earlier times—when populations were smaller, land was less intensively used, and we understood less about our environment—leave us with facilities that are aging and often incapable of serving today's demands. The system is under stress and could be improved.

At the same time, extraordinary advances are being made in electronics, telecommunications, materials, biotechnology, and other fields. These advances have enabled a wide range of new products and processes that improve health, safety, and the quality of life. The nation's infrastructure has changed, but opportunities continue to abound.

We are able to travel farther and more rapidly than former generations, but find ourselves often delayed by traffic and distressed by vehicle-polluted air. We enjoy an unprecedented variety of foods and consumer products, at all seasons and throughout the nation, but regret the despoiling of our lands and waters with residue of packaging and other wastes. We depend on reliable water and energy supplies, and find our cities paralyzed when aging switches fail or pipes burst. In the face of competing social concerns and private needs, we want lower-cost infrastructure. Our infrastructure is not performing at levels its capability and new technology would permit, and can be improved.

New technology—new materials, design methods, controls, operating procedures, maintenance practices, new understanding of how things work and what is needed, and more—these are means for improving infrastructure. Over the past decades, new methods for treating drinking water have vastly improved public health and kept the costs of water low. New traffic control devices have helped relieve congestion, in the face of rapidly increasing auto travel, and have reduced accident rates. New incinerators burn growing volumes of municipal waste, more efficiently and with less air pollution. Much of this new infrastructure technology is a product of research.

RESEARCH AS AN INSTRUMENT FOR IMPROVING INFRASTRUCTURE

Research is a conscious and directed effort to increase our understanding and discover new and better ways to achieve our goals. We see all around us the fruits of modern research, from glass-fiber telecommunications cables to plastic water pipes, from computer-operated transit vehicles to highway pavements using recycled glass. Research has been a wellspring of improvements in America's infrastructure.

This research has been conducted by government agencies, universities, private companies, and public laboratories working in many fields. Millions of dollars have been spent, but the effort pales in comparison with research spending in other fields. Although several professional groups have in recent years established research foundations, total infrastructure research spending remains low. As a nation, we seem increasingly to question the value of research and devote less effort to research for improving infrastructure than the system's scale and significance to our basic well-being warrant.

There are abundant needs and opportunities for infrastructure improvement that research can facilitate. New technologies emerging in the basic sciences may be applied to produce new materials and processes for infrastructure. New patterns of economic and societal activity are shifting the demands for infrastructure's services. New understanding of nature's mechanisms and humans' role is forcing us to expand the range of needs we expect our infrastructure to meet and to reconsider our priorities. We need our infrastructure to provide more services and to do so more effectively.

Many times the research that gains support is undertaken as a response to emergencies. After an earthquake has caused major damage, agencies fund research on methods for repairing bridges that might have been strengthened earlier. When the public outcry grows strident over the apparent health risks posed by toxic wastes, industries search for ways to clean up what might have been prevented. We need to think ahead and anticipate demands of new infrastructure services.

Research is a strategy for working smarter, doing better, and anticipating infrastructure needs. Research can produce infrastructure improvement when it is linked with effective ways to put results into practice. Research leading to infrastructure improvement can enhance our lives. But what specifically should be done, how, and by whom, and how can we do better, are questions that underlie this study. This report presents recommendations for at least a partial answer.

THE STUDY AND ITS ORIGIN

This report documents the results of a study undertaken by a committee of BRB and GEOB. The NSF approached NRC in 1991 to undertake a study to provide advice on the state of the art, basic research needs, and priorities related to the technology of physical infrastructure. BRB, in cooperation with GEOB, established the Committee for an Infrastructure Technology Research Agenda to conduct that study.[3]

The committee held its first meeting on June 29, 1992, and met four additional times during the following 18-month period, to discuss the issues raised by the NSF's request and to develop their recommendations. The committee also sponsored a two-day workshop at the National Academy of Science's Beckman Center in Irvine, California, on June 2 and 3, 1993, to expand the discourse and encourage a broader perspective in the committee's thinking.[4]

The NSF was created to increase the nation's base of scientific and engineering knowledge and strengthen its ability to conduct research in all areas of science and engineering (OFR, 1988). The NSF uses grants, awards, and contracts to initiate and support fundamental, long-term, merit-selected research at universities, nonprofit, and other research organizations.

The NSF's programs have come under intense public scrutiny as policy makers struggle with global competition that threatens U.S. leadership in many areas of science, technology, and the industries that rely on them. Congressional committees and Presidential commissions have concluded that the United States, as a nation, needs to devote more money to R&D[5] in industrial science and technology, to allocate that money more effectively, and to better utilize R&D investments. The NSF has a key role to play in this effort.

The NSF's programs in Structures, Geomechanics, and Building Systems—within the agency's Directorate for Engineering, Division of Mechanical and Structural Systems—support research related to design, construction, maintenance, and operation of civil engineering systems and facilities. This includes research directed at understanding the science and technology of deteriorating infrastructure and actions that can be taken to diagnose, repair, retrofit, and enhance performance of existing facilities.

Since 1991, the Directorate for Engineering has been working with other NSF units to define a program in CIS. The specific scope of CIS and related research are still evolving, but NSF staff have estimated that the NSF is the largest Federal supporter of basic CIS-related research, its $36 million annual spending (1992) accounting for some 65 percent of federal funding in this area (CIS Task Committee, 1993).

THE SCOPE OF INFRASTRUCTURE

In recent years the term "infrastructure" has emerged from technical obscurity to appear frequently in the press. Many people now recognize the word as a shorthand reference to a diverse system of facilities and services, ranging from airports to energy supply to landfills to wastewater treatment. Unlike public works, which it encompasses, the term infrastructure incorporates both physical assets and their economic, social, and political roles, and refers both to public activities and a rich mix of private and joint public-private enterprises. Constructed facilities—infrastructures, as some term them—are at the core of the concept, but are only part of the system.

An earlier NRC committee wrote that infrastructure includes

> ". . . both specific functional modes—highways, streets, roads, and bridges; mass transit; airports and airways; water supply and water resources; wastewater management; solid-waste treatment and disposal; electric

power generation and transmission; telecommunications; and hazardous waste management—and the combined system these modal elements comprise. A comprehension of infrastructure spans not only these public works facilities, but also the operating procedures, management practices, and development policies that interact together with societal demand and the physical world to facilitate the transport of people and goods, provision of water for drinking and a variety of other uses, safe disposal of society's waste products, provision of energy where it is needed, and transmission of information within and between communities."

(NRC, 1987)

To these cited modes may be added public buildings—schools, health care facilities, government offices, and the like—that are linked by the functional systems they house to provide important public services, in much the same fashion as highways and water supply facilities.[6]

For all these elements of infrastructure, the engineering profession is by far the primary source of practitioners, and civil engineering is the leader in numbers of professionals and scope of interests. Much of infrastructure research has been civil engineering research. However, infrastructure calls on other types of engineers, economists, architects, landscape architects, urban planners, public administrators, and professionals in law, medicine, public health and safety, physical sciences, social sciences, and an increasingly broad range of other disciplines.

Failure to acknowledge this broad range of disciplines and issues important to infrastructure leads frequently to large public controversy, high costs, and extensive comment and disruptions, as experienced by the pervasive "NIMBY" response[7] to new technologies and construction. Infrastructure research draws on these disciplines as well. And just as infrastructure professionals have learned that multi-disciplinary teams are needed in planning and design, infrastructure research increasingly must bring together people with diverse backgrounds to pursue a complex common objective.

THE BENEFITS OF INFRASTRUCTURE RESEARCH

Despite the broad scope and diversity of infrastructure, several key common characteristics comprise an intellectual basis for addressing infrastructure as a system and define the benefits research can yield:

1. Infrastructure is, to use the economists' term, "capital intensive," generally involving chiefly materials and equipment rather than labor input, and generally "lumpy," (i.e., capital is required in large concentrations that cannot be finely subdivided). Research can be beneficial by increasing reliable productivity of these capital investments—public assets that serve broad needs in the economy.

2. Infrastructures, long lived and difficult to remove or retire, are routinely designed to meet demands projected for three decades or more into the future. Maintenance and periodic refurbishment are required, but the underlying structure often remains little changed, sometimes for centuries. Even when they are abandoned because they are thought no longer useful (e.g., railroads, and highways in areas of declining population), the facilities themselves are often left in place, too costly to remove. Sometimes the impact is more subtle, but equally long lasting, when systems such as street railways and wired fire-call boxes influence city development patterns, even when the technologies have been replaced. The long design lifetime of infrastructure facilities needs to be reconsidered. Technology for cost-effective down-sizing, adaptive reuse, or retirement and demolition of facilities may be needed. Research can enhance infrastructure flexibility to respond to change—growth, decline, and composition—in the needs for its services.

3. The facilities and users of physical infrastructure are linked in generally complex and geographically extensive networks: roads and interchanges; water treatment plants, supply mains, and distributors; generating plants, transmission lines and step-down transformers; and sewers, treatment plants, and outfalls. These networks stretch over large areas, and often quickly transmit changes from one part of the system to another. Failure of a small element can have drastic consequence for large parts of the system. Research can be beneficial by improving our ability to understand and manage network performance.

4. The various modes of infrastructure are fabricated using primarily Portland cement concrete, steel, and a number of other materials. The characteristics of these traditional materials have changed substantially since initial applications and new materials have been introduced, but ample room for improvement remains. Research can advance understanding of basic behavior of these materials, alone and in the structures they comprise, and of the mechanisms of their manufacture, fabrication, and performance. Their behavior can have broad impact on capability, cost, and durability of individual infrastructures.

5. Infrastructure is valued not primarily for its own sake, but rather as support for other social and economic activities, an encouragement to economic development, or as a short-term source of jobs.[8] A large amount of infrastructure is created because, in economists' terms, it serves demands deriving from these other activities. Demands for reliable water supplies for domestic and industrial use and fire fighting led to the growth of networks of pipes and treatment plants. Demands for flexible and inexpensive movement of people and goods gave rise to roads and highways.

Service demand typically interacts with the facilities and management practices of infrastructure to determine the performance that infrastructure delivers. Principles of economics, political science, sociology, psychology, and other behavioral sciences are primary sources of knowledge about these demands and how they impinge on infrastructure. Research can be beneficial if it enhances our understanding and ability to measure and manage demand for infrastructure services.[9]

6. Because infrastructure facilities are typically large, geographically extensive, and used by many people, infrastructure development and operations often have substantial environmental and social impacts. These impacts have frequently in the past been poorly estimated or neglected in planning and design, and often are badly managed within the context of traditional governmental, economic, and institutional relationships. The role of infrastructure as a factor shaping urban development is only partially described by current theory and statistical studies, as are the economic and social costs of inserting new systems into already developed areas. Research can enhance our ability to avoid or mitigate adverse impacts of infrastructure.

GUIDING PRINCIPLES

Early in their deliberations, the committee realized that their task could be enormous, and that focus would be needed if their work was to be effective. The committee adopted six key assumptions as guiding principles for their subsequent deliberations:

1. The committee considered the NSF's unique role as a source of funds for infrastructure research. The NSF has no direct responsibilities for infrastructure development or management, and is charged to focus on activities intended to add to knowledge rather than to develop marketable products. In asking BRB and GEOB to conduct the study, the NSF requested that the committee focus on the state of the art, basic research needs, and priorities in the technology of physical infrastructure, but within the context of broad national policy issues. The committee thus undertook to identify key research needs and opportunities that could be linked to improved efficiency, effectiveness, and quality of infrastructure facilities and services.

2. Other studies of infrastructure and research agenda-setting efforts[10] provided additional context. Based on the findings of an earlier NRC study,[11] the committee asserted that the NSF would make a great contribution to progress in enhancing the nation's infrastructure by adopting a broad view of infrastructure as an integrated system. This assertion became a basic premise for this study, and led the committee to look beyond its initial scope to a broad range of research needs and opportunities. The artificial disciplinary and institutional divisions among infrastructure modes and

professions are largely historical artifacts that impose barriers to development and adoption of new technology.[12] The NSF can help to lower these barriers by fostering a broader interdisciplinary approach to research. The committee thus agreed to concentrate its attention on R&D that reflects and encourages such an interdisciplinary and intermodal outlook.

3. The committee noted that infrastructure has both private and public aspects. Although current trends toward privatization of some modes while others are shifting toward greater government involvement make it difficult to state a sharp definition of "public," the committee agreed to focus on the public aspects. In this context, "public" conveys meanings related to service to the public, public ownership or operation, and public-sector economics that can be recognized and used to guide—but not to restrict—the scope of the NSF's research programs.

This third assumption notwithstanding, the committee agreed that exchanges of technology between private and public sectors are crucial to the effectiveness of infrastructure R&D. Partnerships of government, academia, and industry are a way to apply limited R&D resources to the search for innovation.

4. The committee agreed that they would focus their attention on infrastructure improvements achievable in the medium-term future (i.e., ten to twenty years hence) in identifying R&D opportunities and assessing priorities. The long physical life and major commitment of public resources embodied in infrastructure make rapid major change in existing networks and patterns of urban development unlikely.[13] New technology is most likely to be adopted if its benefits can be captured without requiring sudden, substantial disruption of existing urban fabric. The medium term is far enough in the future for urban development to evolve through traditional market action, allowing gradual insertion of new infrastructure technology.[14]

5. The committee agreed to accord higher priority to R&D aimed at new infrastructure technology likely to be permissive of alternative future urban development patterns and unlikely to restrict or undermine the viability of existing urban areas. In applying this principle to their work, the committee sought to avoid Utopian schemes and to develop recommendations that are "robust" (i.e., likely to yield substantial payoffs of infrastructure innovation).

6. The committee resolved to exclude from this study any direct consideration of such complex and politically contentious issues as nuclear power and radioactive waste management, large-scale toxic and hazardous waste cleanup, seismic design and risk analysis, and air-pollution control strategies. Such problems are closely allied with infrastructure, but are the target of extensive federal legislation and popular debate. The committee quickly concluded that they had little to add to those discussions.

STRUCTURE OF THE REPORT

This report documents the study and the committee's deliberations and recommendations. The committee intended that its work support the NSF's efforts to define a CIS program, but the committee also looked beyond the immediate scope of the NSF's CIS programs to consider research needs for the nation's infrastructure as a whole. The committee intends its work to offer guidance to the full range of the nation's infrastructure researchers and research sponsors.

Chapter 2 begins with a review of the status of infrastructure research in the United States and the NSF's role in mobilizing and directing U.S. infrastructure research capabilities. Drawing on this background and applying the six principles stated to guide their work, the committee defined seven cross-cutting research niche areas[15] within the broad range of infrastructure technology. These seven niches, essentially clusters of common science and technology issues, the committee judged to be particularly well suited to the NSF's goals and role in research sponsorship. The committee used their descriptions of these seven niches as idea generators for more specific topics for research.[16]

Chapters 3 through 9 describe these seven niches and the committee's suggestions of researchable topics that the NSF and others should address. Taken as a whole, these chapters present a broad scope of basic and strategic infrastructure research that is (1) likely to yield results to fill an identifiable need or bring explicit benefits to development and operation of U.S. infrastructure and (2) appropriate for NSF sponsorship.

The committee considered a wide range of candidate researchable topics to develop their recommendations. These topics were drawn from the review of published reports on infrastructure research needs, committee members' understanding of the needs for U.S. infrastructure improvement (presented in committee meetings and written proposals by individual committee members), and suggestions by participants in the Irvine workshop.

The committee agreed that the topics in Chapters 3 through 9 warrant two approaches. Discipline-based researchers (e.g., mathematicians, economists, materials scientists, and computer software developers) can approach these topics as opportunities to advance and apply their disciplines to the needs of multi-modal infrastructure. At the same time, researchers specialized in the technologies of individual infrastructure modes (e.g., highways, water supply, and municipal solid-waste management) can approach these topics as generalized statements of problems in their traditional fields.

The committee presents these seven niches and the researchable topics comprising each niche area as guidance rather than prescription. The committee acknowledges that many other topics that might have been suggested are missing from Chapters 3 through 9. The typical research questions included within many topic-area descriptions[17] are the committee's suggestions, which individual researchers and research centers may consider in developing programs that match needs and research capabilities. Chapter 10 presents the committee's suggestions regarding how partnerships of researchers and research users, working together, can pursue the cross-cutting philosophy of this agenda.

NOTES

[1]Among the newsworthy recent infrastructure failures were the floodings of downtown Chicago and Washington, D.C., and water-supply contamination in Milwaukee, but perusal of local newspapers reveals many others.

[2]The value of the nation's infrastructure also is uncertain. Estimates by earlier study committees have placed this value in excess of $1.4 trillion (Grant and Lemer, 1993). Statistics published by the Bureau of Economic Analysis, U.S. Department of Commerce indicate total gross value of private and public infrastructure stock (i.e., at investment cost, without depreciation) in 1991 to be at least $3.6 trillion, excluding mining and petroleum and natural gas recovery facilities. Estimates of damage in such recent natural disasters as Hurricane Andrew, the Loma Prieto and Northridge earthquakes, and flooding in the Mississippi River basin suggest that current replacement costs would be even greater.

[3]Biographical sketches of the committee members and staff are presented in Appendix A. Appendix B is the project description, stating the committee's scope of work as initially planned and approved on May 14, 1991, by the Executive Committee of the NRC's Governing Board. The grant agreement between the NRC and the NSF covered the period from December 15, 1991 to May 31, 1994.

[4]Participants in this workshop are listed in Appendix C. A planned second workshop was not held, because of reduced project scope, schedule, and funding considerations (refer to Appendix B).

[5]The distinctions between research and development are often unclear. "Research" generally is characterized on a continuum from "basic," concerned with expansion of knowledge for its own sake, to "applied," aimed at solving practical problems and bringing new products or processes to market. Research seeking new knowledge that may have particular applications but is not market-oriented is sometimes termed "strategic." "Development" occurs at the latter end of the continuum and often extends beyond, into production technology, marketing, and other activities associated with applications of research results in practice. In both common usage and this report, "research" and "R&D" may be used interchangeably.

[6]Public lands—parkland, open space, wilderness areas—could be added. These lands have aesthetic and recreational value, and also (through the work of vegetation and ecologies they support) a role in enhancing supplies of clean air and water. However, the committee determined that these concerns were beyond the scope of its study.

[7]The term "NIMBY," acronym for Not in My Back Yard, has entered the language as a noun, designating unpopular projects as well as public response to such projects.

[8]However, major infrastructure facilities can become important landmarks, community symbols, and cultural icons. The Brooklyn Bridge and Golden Gate Bridge, for example, are valued elements of their communities, with meaning that far exceeds their transportation role. Similarly, for many environmentalists the Glen Canyon Dam epitomizes battles lost.

[9]Political factors also determine how infrastructure is developed. Infrastructure decisions may reflect value choices or distributions of political power, and may not seem economically rational. Research can enhance understanding of the impact of such factors.

[10]Chapter 2 includes a review of a number of such previous agenda-setting efforts.

[11]See Grant and Lemer, 1993.

[12]For an extensive discussion of barriers to technological innovation that affect infrastructure see Dibner and Lemer, 1992.

[13]Some historians have argued that rapid destruction of large parts of urban areas, for example through earthquake, fire, or war, created unique opportunities to introduce new technologies and rapidly upgrade old infrastructure systems. However, patterns of land ownership often survive catastrophe, obstructing change and slowing progress. "Short term" for these systems is probably five to ten years in the future, and systems can last for decades.

[14]Historians have written that widespread conversion from horse-drawn to electric-traction street railways at the end of the nineteenth century, and introduction of sand filters for purifying municipal water supply, occurred in the United States over little more than a decade (Blake, 1956; Nye, 1990).

[15]The committee adopted this term to indicate that other funding agencies might well choose to concentrate their efforts on different sets of topics within the same general framework.

[16]The methods employed in identifying the niche areas and researchable topics within each niche area are summarized in Appendix D.

[17]Typical questions are indicated by bullets (•) in Chapters 3 through 9. In posing these questions, the committee sought to present their ideas in a form that could be readily translated into proposals for research or requests for proposals.

GATEWAY CENTER, UNION STATION, LOS ANGELES

Gateway Center at Union Station is to be a nexus for Los Angeles' burgeoning public transit systems, linking a new metro subway station with suburban bus and light rail lines. The project is inserted into a developed area which had reached a density such that the linkage became essential. Urgency of the scheme was heightened by regional air pollution and traffic congestion problems. With increasing coordination of infrastructure planning and rehabilitation, junctions between subsystems become increasingly important. Significant advantages might be achieved through relocation of compatible elements in common use corridors.

2

THE CONTEXT AND STATUS OF U.S. INFRASTRUCTURE RESEARCH

To be effective, infrastructure research efforts must strike an appropriate balance between need and capability. On the one hand, the research should seek to expand knowledge, fulfill demands, capture opportunities, and gain benefits of applying new technology to U.S. infrastructure. On the other hand, the research should take advantage of available research resources or seek to build new capabilities where needed.

U.S. SPENDING ON INFRASTRUCTURE R&D

Information on the overall level and scope of U.S. effort on infrastructure research, development, and technology adaptation activities is not well developed. Spending occurs in both public and private sectors, and in uncoordinated programs by municipalities and commercial enterprises, as well as large governments or corporations. Some spending occurs to solve problems on a specific project rather than to develop broadly applicable techniques, although lessons learned on a single project often diffuse to projects in other regions. As a part of this study, committee members and staff pieced together available statistics to estimate total U.S. spending for infrastructure research, development, and demonstration.

Since World War II, the U.S. government has become the primary sponsor of all R&D—by one estimate, currently providing about 43 percent of R&D spending in the United States (NSF, 1992b). The Federal government is estimated to be the principal source of infrastructure research spending as well, although only a small portion of the total government R&D funding is devoted to infrastructure. A recent survey conducted by the Civil Engineering Research Foundation (CERF) found this spending to be between $1.026 and $1.386 billion in fiscal year 1992, approximately 1.6 percent of total federal R&D expenditures (CERF, 1993a).

In the CERF study, the NSF was reported to spend less than 10 percent of its $2.7 billion R&D budget on public works infrastructure research. Other reports place total 1993 NSF spending on infrastructure somewhat lower, at $78 million (ENR, 1993).

Drawing on NSF data, the U.S. Congress' Office of Technology Assessment (OTA) reported 1990 federal outlays for public works R&D by five key agencies[1] to have been some $1.4 billion (measured in 1982 dollars) (OTA, 1991), and noted that infrastructure R&D outlays had declined by nearly one-third over the decade from 1980 (in constant dollar terms), a trend that NSF data show to be continuing. Citing National Science Board[2] data, Cohen and Noll (1992) show infrastructure accounting for 1.8 percent of federal R&D appropriations. With such supporting evidence available, the committee adopted $1.026 billion (midpoint of the CERF range) as an estimate of total annual federal infrastructure R&D spending.

Within this total, the allocation of government research funding varies substantially among infrastructure's principal functional modes. At the one extreme, highway research has long been reliably supported by budget allocations from federal and state gasoline tax revenues and is conducted in a large number of federal and state laboratories, universities, and many private companies. At the other extreme, institutional buildings receive little explicit attention as infrastructure, and building research on the whole receives limited funding.

However, the federal government is not the sole source of infrastructure R&D spending. Spending by private-sector firms and not-for-profit organizations on infrastructure research does occur, some of it managed through industry groups such as GRI and EPRI. APWA, AWWA, ASCE, and other professional and trade groups also have research foundations or other units that sponsor and conduct infrastructure-related research. Much of the work of these latter groups is carried out by funding from membership contributions and government contracts and grants.

A variety of private companies is involved in infrastructure-related businesses, including construction, the manufacture of telecommunications and power generating equipment, wire and cable, and chemicals for water treatment, waste processing and disposal, transport and communication services, and instrumentation and software development. These companies spend for both new product development and process improvement.

The construction sector in the United States, a $410 billion industry,[3] is estimated to spend annually only about 0.25 percent of gross sales on research,[4] or $1.025 billion. Much of this research is funded by commercial building-product manufacturers. Only 20 to 25 percent of the total R&D spending is likely devoted to research related to construction of highways, power supply, and other infrastructure.[5] These figures imply that annual infrastructure R&D spending by the construction industry is about $230 million (midpoint of the range).

Manufacturing related to infrastructure, but not to construction products and materials, includes primarily transportation, communications, and power generation and equipment. These industries may spend as much as $3 billion annually on R&D. However, some two-thirds of this amount is attributable to the motor vehicle and aircraft manufacturers, much of it for new model development. Perhaps 20 percent of the total, $600 million, may be directed toward achieving substantive infrastructure systems innovation.

The contribution of transportation and public utilities businesses to the U.S. gross national product (GNP) was approximately $440 billion in 1988 (DOC, 1991). If perhaps 0.02 percent of sales are devoted by such businesses to infrastructure-related R&D,[6] then the estimated annual spending is $88 million.

Various private firms provide design services, construction management, operations research, and other professional services related to infrastructure. United States firms annually perform some $30 billion in domestic and overseas design and related work, of which approximately half is related to infrastructure (ENR, 1992). Such firms typically conduct informal in-house R&D for new product development and may compete for government-sponsored research funds, spending in aggregate less than 0.05 percent of sales on R&D, or an estimated $15 million annually.

Much of this spending is associated with civil engineering and related professions. U.S. government 1991 budgetary obligations for civil engineering research totaled $55 million, some two-thirds of which was to be spent under NSF programs (NSF, 1992b; CERF, 1993c). Perhaps $22 million, less than half of the total amount, is targeted on areas specifically related to infrastructure. This amount, probably included in the previously mentioned CERF and OTA estimates of government-funded infrastructure research, may be representative of levels of private spending, reinforcing the previous estimate.

Combining these several estimates, the total annual U.S. R&D spending on infrastructure-related technology may be approximately $2.1 billion, as summarized in Table 2. This amount is approximately 1.6 percent of total estimated U.S. R&D spending.

Members of the infrastructure professional, academic, and research communities have expressed concern that these spending levels are too low and that evidence is strong that declining research underlies in part a purported lag in technological innovation in the field. However, the data are poor, the topic is complex, and such relationships are difficult to demonstrate. Further, many analysts have pointed out that R&D activity does not necessarily lead to innovation.[7]

Nevertheless, the committee agreed that low research effort signals an environment less likely to yield innovation, and evidence suggests that the United States may be lagging in comparison to other countries. For example, Cohen and Noll (1992) noted that the United States spends comparatively less on civilian technology than other advanced, industrialized nations. Taken as defined by the reporting government agencies, infrastructure R&D priority is similar in the United States, Germany, Japan, and Britain, but is a notably higher priority in France (see Table 3).

However, the definitions of what comprises infrastructure R&D in these countries is not necessarily similar. Taken together, environment, energy, and "infrastructure" R&D spending account for approximately 6

TABLE 2 Estimated Infrastructure Research Spending in the United States, 1992 (Sources: Committee estimates, CERF, and NSF)

Source of funds	Estimated annual amount
Federal Government	$1,206 million
Private Sector	
Construction Industry	230 "
Equipment Manufacturers	600 "
Transportation and Utility Service Companies	88 "
Design Construction Management, and Other Service Companies	15 "
Total Infrastructure R&D Spending	$2,139 million

TABLE 3 International Comparison of Infrastructure Research Spending (Source: Cohen and Noll, 1992)

	Distribution of Government Research Budgets by Percentage (1987)			
Country	Infrastructure	Environment	Energy	Defense
U.S.	1.8	0.5	3.6	68.6
France	3.2	0.4	6.7	34.1
Germany	1.9	3.3	8.7	12.5
Japan	1.8	0.5	23.2	4.5
Britain	1.5	1.0	3.5	50.3

percent of R&D spending in the United States and Britain, and about 10 to 14 percent in France and Germany. In Japan, which has no significant domestic energy resources, the total is over 25 percent.

Table 3 data seem to match observers' impressions of the infrastructure R&D activities in these countries. Participants in reconnaissance visits sponsored by CERF and the NSF have returned with tales of extensive research facilities and far-ranging programs (CERF, 1991b; NSF, 1992a). Others have pointed to such examples as the French telecommunications system, Japanese precision construction, and Swiss bridge design as demonstrations of the payoffs of greater effort on R&D and willingness to apply new technology to infrastructure.

RESEARCHERS AND RESEARCH INSTITUTIONS

The pattern of who does research and how their results are applied differs substantially among countries, and this variation clearly has impact on the productivity of R&D spending. In the United States, R&D funding is spent at government laboratories, universities, quasi-governmental laboratories,[8] and private research organizations; and much of this spending is directed at investigating specific problems encountered in practice.

Government Laboratories

The federal government has developed several R&D centers to support agencies' infrastructure-related missions. The U.S. Army Corps of Engineers, for example, is responsible for navigable waterways, flood control, hydropower, and other water resources, as well as for military programs, operates the Construction Engineering Research Laboratory in Illinois and the Waterways Experiment Station in Mississippi. The Department of Transportation has research facilities in Virginia (highways), New Jersey (air transportation), and Massachusetts (transportation systems). The Bureau of Reclamation conducts and manages research from its Denver headquarters. Similarly, the Department of Energy, the Environmental Protection Agency, the Department of Agriculture's Forest Products Service, and others maintain R&D operations that work on infrastructure topics.

Several of the laboratories operate at least partially as contracting organizations, entering into project agreements to investigate specific problems faced by the program elements of their agencies. These laboratories depend on funding provided by the operating programs rather than direct budget allocations for research, and thus have limited ability to set their own research agendas.

Academic Institutions

Within academic institutions, government and private research laboratories,[9] and private companies, research and development activities applied to infrastructure are performed largely under the auspices of civil engineering programs or units associated with development and management of public works. Programs in electrical, mechanical, water resources, and construction engineering, architecture, urban planning, urban design, and landscape architecture also readily include topic-related infrastructure systems and technology. In addition, the fields of economics, public finance, public administration, geography, and regional planning contribute regularly to enhanced understanding and methodology for infrastructure development and management.

Most of this work and the centers where it occurs are mode-specific (e.g., transportation or electric power). However, in recent years, several universities and other groups have established research centers under the title of "infrastructure." These include a consortium of New York City area institutions led by Columbia University; a research center at Northwestern University;[10] a joint venture of Harvard's Taubman Center for State and Local Government and the Graduate School of Public Affairs of the University of Colorado at Denver; separate and unrelated programs at the University of Nebraska, the Massachusetts Institute of Technology, George Mason University, and the New Jersey Institute of Technology. However, it is the committee's sense that the absence of either a national institutional focus or reliable funding for research on infrastructure as a whole has limited the ability of such centers to develop broad capabilities. Their programs remain generally small, unrelated to one another except through collegial communication, and opportunistic in their pursuit of research funding and their consequent research agendas.

Professional, Industry, and Trade Institutes

Several professional associations and industry groups have formed research institutes that sponsor or undertake infrastructure-related research. Some of the more prominent of these organizations are listed in Table 4. Most of these organizations depend for funding on membership fees and voluntary contributions, and contracts or grants from government agencies, foundations, and private corporations.

The electric power and natural gas industries have established EPRI and GRI to conduct research. EPRI is funded through voluntary contributions from member utilities (NRC, 1989a). GRI is funded by surcharges on the rates charged by interstate pipelines for gas for resale and transportation. These surcharges would be passed on through the distribution com-

TABLE 4 Selected Research Organizations Associated with Professional and Trade Associations

American Consulting Engineers Council Research & Management Foundation
American Concrete Institute Concrete Research Council
American Architectural Foundation
American Public Works Association Research Foundation
American Society of Mechanical Engineers Center for Research and Technology Development
American Water Works Association Research Foundation
Civil Engineering Research Foundation
Construction Industry Institute
Electric Power Research Institute
Gas Research Institute
Landscape Architecture Foundation
National Association of Home Builders National Research Center
Urban Land Institute
Water Environment Research Foundation

panies to the ultimate consumers (NRC, 1989b). Seeking to emulate the federal gasoline tax set-aside that supports much of the nation's highway research, membership fees are based on the annual revenues of the member companies, which are generally proportional to the kilowatt-hours of electric power or cubic feet of gas produced and sold.

International Activities[11]

As in the United States, most infrastructure research in other countries is directed at specific modes and concentrated in government agencies, but is funded directly by the national governments to a much greater extent than in this country. However, a few foreign programs are multimodal in scope. Most notable is Sweden, where the University of Umea, the Royal Institute of Technology, and other universities have been involved in research on infrastructure related to regional development, primarily with Swedish government funding. Research on technological innovation, focused primarily on transport infrastructure, and on global climate change (with some attention to the influence of infrastructure) has been conducted at the International Institute for Applied Systems Analysis in Austria. Japanese industry, universities, and government have been pursuing several initiatives to explore new urban infrastructure systems, under the guidance of the Ministry of Construction and Ministry of International Trade and Industry. The National Research Council of Canada, a government agency, has also undertaken programs of infrastructure research.

The World Bank, with lending programs operating in some 60 nations and 200 cities worldwide, has sponsored a wide range of research on infrastructure, emphasizing technologies appropriate for application in regions with low income or at early stages of industrialization. The Bank seeks to define more clearly the links between infrastructure investment and economic development to provide sound bases for their lending programs.

PRIOR STUDIES OF RESEARCH NEEDS

These various research sponsors and researchers have, from time to time, undertaken to define infrastructure research needs statements, to direct their own activities, or to have broader influence within the research establishment. The committee found that few of these past efforts were comprehensive, aimed at infrastructure as a multi-functional system of facilities and services. Most such studies were developed to deal with one mode alone, such as highways or water supply. In view of the structure of infrastructure, such a modal focus is not surprising.

For example, a study funded by the Federal Highway Administration and conducted by the Transportation Research Board produced an agenda for highway research focused on what might be termed "hard" technology, such as asphalt behavior, highway deicing technology, and bridge deck performance. The report, *America's Highways: Accelerating the Search for Innovation* (TRB, 1984) recommended a program of such research that became the basis for the Congressionally-funded Strategic Highway Research Program (SHRP), a five-year activity administered by NRC. The SHRP, ending in 1993, did in fact produce many useful results, and the Federal Highway Administration is establishing a national training center for state officials, intended to speed transfer of SHRP-produced technology into practice in the 50 states.

The committee did review some studies that were based on a broader perspective of infrastructure, although not necessarily aimed explicitly at developing research agendas. One such study, exploring the development of a national urban policy (NRC, 1984), held a symposium entitled The Adequacy and Maintenance of Urban Public Facilities, that identified an extensive research agenda, including the implications for technology development for new and existing infrastructures. The cross-cutting infrastructure research topics addressed primarily management and economic needs, such as the role of standards and risk analysis in infrastructure decision making, life-cycle cost analysis strategies for infrastructure maintenance and repair, methods for evaluating benefits and costs of various levels of system performance, and effective diffusion of innovation into practice. One paper presented in the report calls for research on condition assessment methods and the value of information systems in condition assessment.

Another NRC study (NRC, 1985), not directly related to this earlier work, included a workshop that attempted to identify technological alternatives—new systems, materials, and devices—for future replacement of present urban infrastructure systems. What emerged from the workshop was a call for further research on the integration of various infrastructure elements. Workshop papers described cross-cutting research areas such as communications, broadly used to describe the use of new electronic technologies (e.g., computerized mapping and modeling, telematics, remote measurement technologies, automated decision and control systems, and integrated computer systems). Others considered ways to combine infrastructure functions.

The National Council on Public Works Improvement (NCPWI) 1988 report, *Fragile Foundations,* was a broad assessment of the nation's infrastructure systems, that included considerations of the needs and opportunities for research (NCPWI, 1988). An NRC-conducted study supporting the NCPWI's work advocated integrated or cross-cutting infrastructure research and innovation as well as modal research. While the report does not present an agenda for such cross-cutting research, it did target four areas of opportunity, in materials science, information technology, nondestructive evaluation, and urban and regional planning (NRC, 1987).

The National Academy of Engineering sponsored a workshop in 1986, on The Evolution of Future Infrastructure. Workshop papers were subsequently published as a report reviewing the technology, history, and theory of infrastructure. A paper by Ibbs and Echeverry (1988) concentrates on cross-cutting technologies for more efficient construction, referring particularly to new materials technology, new monitoring and sensing technologies, nondestructive testing, new construction methods, construction robotics, new management technologies, and data bases for management.

An extensive discussion of infrastructure research is contained in an OTA report on the federal role in infrastructure policy (OTA, 1990). This report includes a chapter on cross-cutting technologies for infrastructure, identifying several technologies on which research would be appropriate:

- measurement, instrumentation, and nondestructive evaluation;
- information and decision systems, including maintenance management information systems, geographic information systems, artificial intelligence, and simulation models;
- communications and positioning systems, including signal systems and the use of satellites;
- field construction technologies, including trenchless construction technologies, tunnels, soil improvements and stabilization, dredging technology, and rail track construction and rehabilitation;
- materials and corrosion, including continued research on concrete, asphalt, steel, geotextiles, plastics, advanced composites, and research on protecting materials against corrosion; and

- technology management, including project design, procurement options, standards and specifications, risk and reliability, proprietary technologies, and personnel training, education, and recruitment.

Revitalization of public works infrastructure was one of five thrust areas at the 1991 Civil Engineering Research Needs Forum held in Washington, D.C., by CERF. Participants in that forum identified and ranked 10 high-priority research topics (CERF, 1991a):

1. developing tools to make intelligent management decisions;
2. finding new ways to finance infrastructure investments;
3. extending the useful life of the infrastructure;
4. protecting bridges from natural hazards;
5. identifying structural problems by diagnosis;
6. removing institutional barriers to innovation;
7. economic benefits from public works investments;
8. improving water-resource systems data through new technology;
9. mitigating coastal damage from natural hazards; and
10. protecting dams against earthquakes and floods.

Estimates were made of appropriate levels of spending on each topic. The third item, extending the useful life of the infrastructure, was estimated to warrant some $100 million in research spending, more than 10 times the allocation to any other topic. More recently, CERF has proposed establishment of a research program in high-performance materials (CERF, 1993b).

These various statements of infrastructure research needs bear great similarities, particularly in their emphasis on materials, condition assessment, and monitoring, and applications of newly developed electronics and information management technologies to traditional infrastructure. A shift in emphasis from construction of new facilities to maintenance and repair of existing ones pervades the final decades of the twentieth century, and is reflected in these studies. The committee considered this shift and these previous research needs studies in their own deliberations.

THE NSF'S ROLE IN INFRASTRUCTURE RESEARCH

The NSF's support of research is meant to build a knowledge base of engineering and science to support technological innovation throughout the nation's economy. Because the NSF's research spending is concentrated in the nation's colleges and universities, its impact extends beyond immediate research results to the next generation of infrastructure professionals.

The NSF's independence and freedom from association with any particular infrastructure mode or interest group means that the Foundation's spending can be directed in a neutral and nonproprietary manner. In the

BATTERY PARK CITY, LOWER MANHATTAN, NEW YORK

The 100-acre Battery Park City was built chiefly on dredged sand hydraulic fill over organic silt on the Hudson River waterfront. Pre-planning of the infrastructure elements, ganged on pile-supported roadway platforms or on stabilized fill, allowed the site to be subdivided for various development modes. These included smaller groupings, forming in effect, intimate city neighborhoods. These environmental and social impacts have frequently been poorly estimated or neglected in planning and design. The role of infrastructure as a factor shaping urban development is poorly understood, as are the economic and social costs of inserting new systems into already developed areas. Research can enhance our ability to avoid or mitigate adverse impacts of infrastructure.

past, this spending has been allocated and administered primarily along disciplinary lines, matched to the structure of academic institutions that are the NSF's primary grant recipients.

However, from time to time, special programs have been undertaken that encourage collaboration across academic disciplinary boundaries or that address needs not easily placed within traditional organizational structures. For example, over the past several years the NSF has funded initiation of several research centers, focused on earthquake engineering, Portland-cement-concrete technology, and large-scale structures. These centers typically bring together faculty and students from several parts of the university—or even from several universities—to work on projects housed within the center's administrative structure. The housing may be physical as well, with offices, equipment, and meeting areas providing a base of operations and sense of identity for the center's activities.

Within the context of the NSF's traditional role and the complexity of U.S. infrastructure needs, a CIS (Civil Infrastructure Systems)[12] Task Group recommended (NSF, 1993) a "Research and Knowledge Transfer Program . . . to enhance system performance and the longevity for existing and future infrastructure systems." The recommendation encompassed research in three broad topic areas—deterioration science, assessment technologies, and renewal engineering—intended to support this aim, and knowledge-transfer efforts to encourage practical application of research results (Table 5). Subsequent planning has added a fourth topic, institutional effectiveness and productivity. These NSF task-group recommendations were part of the context for the committee's work.

The NSF's CIS program is being developed for application over the next several years to address currently well-recognized needs for better understanding of facilities aging, maintenance, and repair. The research niches presented in this report are intended to extend beyond the CIS pro-

TABLE 5 CIS Program Elements Recommended by the NSF Task Group (NSF, 1993)[13]

RESEARCH
Deterioration science
Assessment technologies
Renewal engineering
KNOWLEDGE TRANSFER
Proof-of-concept projects
Education, workshops, seminars
Expert systems, information systems, publications
International cooperation

gram as it is being defined, to look toward needs emerging over the coming 10 to 20 years and to consider the full range of services and facilities that comprise the nation's infrastructure.

Many needs for infrastructure research have to do with processes (e.g., for waste treatment, energy transmission, and control of leachates) outside the scope of NSF programs that sponsored the committee's work. The committee generally sought to maintain a focus on the structures and technologies that support or house such processes, rather on than the processes themselves.[14]

Both the CIS program and this broader scope of research build on current practice and previous research. The task facing the committee was not simply to judge what are significant questions for which research might find answers, but rather what are the questions that particularly warrant research that might be funded by the NSF, alone and with other agencies. Such questions will comprise the niches, within the broad scope of infrastructure research, that will be the most appropriate application of NSF 's inevitably limited resources.

THE NICHE AREAS

These niches represent broad cross-cutting areas for research wherein the NSF's sponsorship is likely to be particularly productive. Research topics within these niche areas would represent an intersection of current and anticipated infrastructure need and the NSF's mission and capability, within a broader context of the U.S. infrastructure research establishment.

The scope of the committee's deliberations was set to address, if not resolve, a tension between committee members' tendencies toward broad systems generality and reductionist specificity. The former tendency, growing out of recognition of the complexity of infrastructure and its urban settings, encouraged broadly stated research questions and expansive programs. The latter tendency reflected desires to assure that the research is practical and aimed at feasible targets. Both stances have merit, and striking the appropriate balance attracted continuing discussion as the committee defined and refined its guidance in these seven broad infrastructure research niche areas:

- *Systems life-cycle management,* including plant or network operations, asset deployment, maintenance practices, system performance assessment, and control, management, renewal decisions, quality of life and environmental management, throughout all stages of the life cycle from initial materials production to final facility demolition and waste disposal;
- *Analysis and decision tools,* for planning and design, needs assessment, dealing with capacity issues;

• *Information management,* including data collection, storage, assessment, and retrieval in forms that support decision making;

• *Condition assessment and monitoring technology,* for facilities and service performance (e.g., flow metering and effluent content);

• The *science of materials performance and deterioration,* including mechanical and chemical behavior, changes with time and use, and so on;

• *Construction equipment and procedures,* including construction management methodology; and

• *Technology management,* such as selection of treatment process or transport mode, bases for decision making, and environmental or social consequences.

The committee found that boundaries among broad niche areas are inexact and difficult to define. There is sometimes overlap or duplication among specific topics and research questions presented in different niche areas. Such overlap results not only because infrastructure technology is complex and multidisciplinary, but also because there is generally more than one way to look at each problem. Similar topics may be stated from several perspectives, each of which may lead to different research approaches, different likelihoods of success, and possibly different results. One approach to a problem may yield useful results where another does not. Also, because research sometimes yields unexpected and serendipitous results, variety increases the potential scope for discovery. Hence, variety may be a key characteristic of a robust research agenda.

NOTES

[1]The Departments of Interior and Transportation, Environmental Protection Agency, Army Corps of Engineers, and National Institute of Standards and Technology.

[2]The National Science Board advises and governs NSF activities.

[3]In terms of 1987 value of new construction put in place (DOC, 1991).

[4]Such statistics are not readily available. This and subsequent estimates are based on cited data or studies, or reflect the judgement of committee members and staff.

[5]By comparison, approximately one-third of total annual construction spending is typically devoted to public works and private infrastructure facilities (BRB, 1988).

[6]This is a typical percentage in many industries, but well below such research-intensive industries as pharmaceuticals or microelectronics.

[7]For a discussion of technological innovation, as it occurs in the construction-related industries, refer to Dibner and Lemer (1992).

[8]Such institutions as the Argonne National Laboratories and the MITRE Corporation were founded as adjuncts to government agencies and still enjoy a special status in their access to government R&D funding.

[9]Including both government agencies, such as the National Institute of Standards and Technology (NIST) and the Army's Construction Engineering Research Laboratory (CERL), and private or quasi-governmental institutions such as Battelle Institute.

[10]The Northwestern Infrastructure Technology Institute was designated as one of several recipients of funds earmarked for university transportation centers, under the Intermodal Surface Transportation Efficiency Act of 1992.

[11]The committee did not conduct a formal survey of international infrastructure research. Committee members and staff were familiar with infrastructure research programs ongoing in many countries, including findings from reconnaissance trips sponsored by the NSF and CERF.

[12]The term encompasses essentially the same scope of infrastructure as was initially posed for this present study. As previously explained, the study committee took a somewhat broader view.

[13]A fourth research area, on institutional effectiveness and productivity (encompassing economic, labor force, and human capital issues), was added in subsequent planning. In addition, other NSF funding for science, mathematics, and engineering could be applied to infrastructure-related topics.

[14]A committee member noted that in the nuclear power industry this distinction is sometimes termed the "balance of plant" (i.e., everything outside of the reactor vessel).

RECONSTRUCTION OF CROTON LAKE GATEHOUSE, NEW YORK

The landmarked gatehouse structure for the main New York City reservoir had to be rehabilitated at this prominent site and an expansion unit incorporated into the design. The challenge was to use new materials in a style compatible with that of the historic structure to create a symbol for the entire system. The challenge is embodied in questions for research, for example, "What are likely ranges of service lives for recycled or reprocessed materials, components, and facilities, considering both compatibility of these materials with existing facilities and application in new facilities?"

3

SYSTEMS LIFE-CYCLE MANAGEMENT

Management of infrastructure as a multifunctional system, expected to provide and support a wide range of services over an extended period of time, represents a radical departure from past practices that have focused on individual modes (e.g., highways or water supply) and on sequential stages of facility development. Research is needed to enable day-to-day decision making to reflect the complexity inherent in this system concept.

The complexity stems from the hierarchy of activities (e.g., from establishing basic goals setting the operating procedures for each functional element), uncertainties in demands placed on the system by users and neighbors, evolution in technologies, and relationships among institutions. The complexity stems also from gaps in knowledge. There is no generally accepted definition of good performance that spans the range of infrastructure.[1] There are few methods for exploring the tradeoffs among ways to meet service demands, through resource distribution among infrastructure modes or by influencing demands rather than service supply. There is little reliable guidance for how best to introduce new technology without unduly adverse social or environmental impacts.

Research to make this complexity more manageable is necessarily multidisciplinary. Such topics as human settlement patterns; "opportunity costs"[2] of pre-emptive actions such as reserving rights-of-way for future systems; impacts of infrastructure on adjacent communities and lands; interactions among transport, telecommunications, and other infrastructures, as well as distributions of costs and benefits among groups of people in a region, among regions, and among present and future generations, call for research contributions from the social, political, economic, and physical sciences.

The committee proposes that the NSF should foster research to enhance fundamental understanding of the long-term role of infrastructure as a contributor to the quality of life in cities, suburbs, and other developed areas, one that can be more effectively managed in design, construction, and operations. Three primary topic areas offering high payoff potential are discussed in this chapter:

(1) enhancing knowledge of the sources of infrastructure demand and how demand interacts with the system to influence service life to enable development of more effective infrastructure management tools and procedures;

(2) data collection and information-analysis tools to support total-system inventory and coordinated management of infrastructure within a metropolitan area; and

(3) analyses of standards, regulations, and other external factors (e.g., political and social values, and technological advances) that influence infrastructure performance and service life.

INFRASTRUCTURE DEMAND AND SERVICE-LIFE MANAGEMENT

A basis for many infrastructure facility design decisions is that the facility will be in service for a period of 25 to 50 years. In practice, infrastructures are often kept in service much longer, and these aging facilities are frequently found to be poorly suited to current demands. It is frequently found that these long-lived facilities are poorly suited to current demands. The system generally lacks flexibility to adjust. This is particularly true for underground facilities, where initial costs are very high and repair or replacement are very difficult.

The demand for infrastructure depends on a wide range of economic and social activities, environmental constraints, technological options, and societal priorities. For example, the volume and characteristics of municipal solid wastes that ultimately are deposited in landfills or dumped in the oceans depend on patterns of human consumption and how wastes are processed at intermediate stages (e.g., volume reduction, segregation by type, and recycling). Incinerators produce air pollutants and ash that may be considered hazardous, which in turn create new disposal demands. Landfills present possible soil and groundwater pollution hazards.

Similar chains of demand, which may be cited for all infrastructure modes, change over time and are not generally well understood. However, over the course of the infrastructure's service life, the value of activities that depend on the infrastructure's services is very large. Seemingly small gains or losses in productivity caused by infrastructure performance can accumulate into very large impacts on an area's economy and quality of life.

Research on this set of issues concerns explorations of the factors influencing infrastructure demand and how demand interacts with the system to affect service life. The urgency of this research is high because infrastructure capacity limitations currently are being encountered in many areas. Government budgetary deficits that restrict new investment make capacity expansion difficult, increasing the need for management of demand, enhancement of capacity through operations, or both.

The benefits to be gained through research in these areas include more effective infrastructure management tools and procedures that can be used to enhance infrastructure performance at lower costs. Research on the life expectancy of infrastructures—through analysis and characterization of components and subsystems—can improve infrastructure managers' predictions and thereby foster better decisions about facilities operation, maintenance, repair, or replacement. Research on demand can improve managers' abilities to achieve a better match between existing systems and the demands placed on those systems.

Issues of Public Goods Demand, Prices, and Costs

Infrastructure's services fall generally into the category economists' term "public goods," for which prices that can be charged seldom cover the costs of production. Understanding the allocation of public costs and benefits, excessive demand spurred by low prices, network economies,[3] and distortions of markets for other goods and services that use infrastructure are among the areas that warrant continuing research. New measurement and communications technologies that facilitate continuous in-house metering of water and power consumption, automated vehicle tracking and toll collection, and other innovative charging mechanisms can enhance the manager's ability to compute and reflect full costs in infrastructure service pricing.

Typical questions for research might include the following examples:

- What are the full costs of infrastructure services, and how are these costs distributed?
- Can depletion allowances, extraction subsidies, and other new price-modification mechanisms be adapted to modify demand for municipal solid waste disposal services?
- How can infrastructure prices be adjusted to respond to variations in demand (e.g., by time of day, day of week, or season) to achieve more efficient utilization of facilities?

Managing Derived Demand

Much of the demand for infrastructure is derived from other economic and social activities (e.g., municipal disposal of wastes from consumption, and transportation as a means to get to work or deliver goods for manufacturing). Influencing the patterns of demand for goods and services, from which demands for infrastructure are derived, is potentially a way of influencing infrastructure demand levels and operating efficiency. The "energy crisis" of the 1970s motivated increased interest in car-pooling and "flexitime" among workers as ways of managing highway usage. Droughts in western U.S. states have spurred increased water recycling and limitations on water use for domestic irrigation (e.g., watering the lawn). Research on this topic could encompass both regulatory and pricing strategies, as well as explorations of the sociology and psychology of personal habits and cultural patterns that are nonprice determinants of demand.

Typical questions for research might include the following examples:

- Are regulatory tools effective in the long term for suppressing or redistributing peak-period infrastructure demand?
- How have land-use policies influenced infrastructure investment and performance levels?
- How does infrastructure investment influence land-development intensity and subsequent demand for infrastructure?
- How do the values underlying public expressions of environmental concerns influence use and willingness to pay for infrastructure?

Infrastructure as a Life-Cycle Production Process

While infrastructure in use provides services that support other activities, the preponderance of infrastructure research concerns development and management of facilities. Further, these facilities require substantial inputs of materials that in turn are major consumers of energy and other resources. Research is warranted to characterize more effectively the processes for production of infrastructure services, viewed on a basis of the total life-cycle of the inputs. Inputs would include clean air and water and other environmental quality elements, as well as labor and construction materials. Research would include modeling of technologies and tracing the chains of input and output from initial materials production through demolition or redeployment of obsolete facilities. New data collection methods (e.g., geographic information systems [GIS] and aerial and satellite imaging), applied to monitoring of operating systems, could enable the methods of statistical inference to be applied more broadly and could yield valuable results.

Typical questions for research might include the following examples:

- What are the relative life-cycle supply resource efficiencies of alternative infrastructure technologies (e.g., rail transit versus guideway bus versus conventional highway, water supply by greywater[4] collection, and recycling versus conventional extraction and treatment)?

- How do infrastructure marginal costs respond at the system level to changes in land-use management practices and subarea abandonments?
- Can renewable biological materials (e.g., wood products) be more widely and advantageously applied in infrastructure?
- Are service-life assumptions being used in planning and design (e.g., materials durability, economic discount rates, and demand levels) distorting decisions in consistent ways?

Assessing Consequences of Materials Innovation

R&D on new materials—products of molecular-level engineering, composites, modified Portland cements, and others (see Chapter 8)—with high strength-to-weight and strength-to-cost ratios offer opportunities for radically improved infrastructure designs. Increasing incentives for recycling and waste minimization may require new reprocessing technologies and materials selection to facilitate reprocessing. The potential consequences of such changes, for infrastructure service lifetimes, reliability, capacity to meet unexpected high demand, and maintenance practices, could be far-reaching and warrant research.

Typical questions for research might include the following examples:

- What are likely ranges of service lives for recycled or reprocessed materials, components, and facilities, considering both compatibility of these materials with existing facilities and application in new facilities?
- How might the maintenance needs of future infrastructure differ from today's, in terms of skilled labor, special equipment and procedures, new materials, and other resources?

TOTAL SYSTEM INVENTORY, MONITORING, AND MANAGEMENT

No comprehensive database exists on the composition and condition of U.S. infrastructure systems; nor do many metropolitan areas have such data. Some modes, such as highways, have been relatively well inventoried and records are regularly updated. Other systems (e.g., urban water supply) in many areas contain elements that were constructed decades ago, and historical design and construction records (sometimes including even their locations) have been effectively lost.

The lack of such data presents obvious challenges to infrastructure managers, as evidenced by accidental damages and unexpected high costs when infrastructures are being repaired. However, the same lack of data also poses substantial barriers to development of effective and reliable tools for predicting infrastructure service life.

Data alone do not enable more effective analysis or decision making. Methods are needed to gain easy access to data and convert them into useful information. These methods must be able to deal with data and information at various levels of detail and aggregation (e.g., facilities and networks, local and regional), and referring to different ages and geographic areas. Data access, presentation, and security must be considered to make infrastructure information usable by a wide range of people in a wide range of private and public ownership and management settings. Highlighting and dealing with tradeoffs among conflicting objectives, a central part of infrastructure decision making, must be facilitated by good information.

The scope of research in this area can be very broad: measurement devices, computer hardware and software; systems modeling, optimization methods, statistical analysis; database development and management, information display; historical studies, decision rules; and institutional structures. These are only a few of the sources of research questions. Research in this area, aimed at the needs of decision making, is closely related to research in the general area of information management (Chapter 6) and condition monitoring and assessment technologies (Chapter 7) adapted to infrastructure. Because the results of such work can contribute to more effective decision making, the payoffs of research in this area are closely allied to those concerning demand and service-life management. In contrast to that area, however, research directed at program elements, such as those discussed in this section, will typically involve substantial amounts of field observation of facilities in service.

Analytical Inventories of Infrastructure Systems

Complete inventories of a region's infrastructure, even when they exist, are often in forms poorly suited to technical analysis and comprehensive management. Integrated databases are needed to support development of predictive models, estimations of reliability and risk levels, and in-service performance monitoring. In many cases, compilation of existing data will require assembly of diverse historic documents from several government agencies and jurisdictions particularly at local government levels. Development of such inventories may not warrant NSF support as a singular objective, but would form important elements of a broader infrastructure research program in a region. Advancement of data collection and management capabilities such as three-dimensional computer graphics and GIS, satellite imaging, and remote sensing technologies could be pursued.

Typical questions for research might include the following examples:

- What protocols should be adopted for data collection and storage for integrated infrastructure databases?

- How can three-dimensional and seasonal geographically based data be most effectively displayed to support integrated infrastructure analysis and decision making?
- What historical data (e.g., socioeconomic and hydrologic) should be maintained in disaggregated form to support future research in other fields (e.g., urban development, history, and natural hazard assessment)?

Statistical Analyses and Benchmarking[5] of Infrastructure

Descriptive statistics on age, composition, and other characteristics of infrastructure systems are important indicators of likely future problems and needs. Research to determine performance benchmarks and trends can help to establish investment and repair priorities and to estimate program costs. To some extent, such work has been partially done for highway bridges and to assess dam safety. For example, plastics have been used extensively in water and gas distribution systems for several decades, but there has been no comprehensive assessment of their in-service performance, nor are there reliable predictive models for their characterization and long-term behavior.

Similarly, acidic rainwater may be causing corrosion and reduced expected service lives of infrastructures, but statistics on the scale of the problem are not available. Research on this topic could include field sampling of infrastructure performance and statistical estimation of service parameters.

Typical questions for research might include the following examples:

- What portions of the infrastructure system are being exposed to service conditions that are changing substantially and that differ from design assumptions?
- Can performance of the several infrastructure modes be characterized on common scales to determine whether costs and effectiveness are in balance throughout the system?

Deviations-Detection Systems for Public Health and Safety

Comprehensive data and benchmarking of performance will facilitate effective monitoring of infrastructure service conditions and, in combination with new detection and communications technologies, enhance ability to respond to deviations that signal threats to public health or safety or to service continuity. Research on this topic might explore early epidemiological warning systems for environmental hazards as well as alarm systems for infrastructure operators. Improving accident or hazard management might involve closer linking of police, fire, health, and infrastructure operations and maintenance personnel through an active sensor network, perhaps supported by on-line knowledge-based expert system programs to assist in determining best response measures.

Typical questions for research might include the following examples:

- Are there generic rules that should be followed for optimal evacuation or congestion clearance and subsequent flow rerouting within infrastructure networks, when accident or failure has taken links out of service?
- Can improvements be made in matching infrastructure demands to network capacities during periods of peak demand, such that overall performance is improved?
- How should users' and operators' perspectives on hazard and risk influence appropriate response when new potential hazards are identified?

Quicker Response Infrastructure Management

The allowable time interval for management to respond to changes in system conditions is shrinking. Research is needed to explore fundamental changes that may be necessary in infrastructure system organization and management to avoid increasing instability. Such research may advance technologies for SCADA.[6] Technical innovations (e.g., imbedded sensors linked to a pro-active control center), innovative cost-sharing methods and other management tools, and new institutional arrangements for infrastructure management would be appropriate to this topic.

Typical questions for research might include the following examples:

- Do reductions of redundancy and dispersion (e.g., from increased use of fiber optic cables, rail transit, or other high line-capacity technologies) require changes in system management to maintain infrastructure performance?
- Are current response times and strategies for dealing with infrastructure disturbances appropriate and optimal, in terms of costs and potential avoidable losses?
- How do infrastructure management practices, including recurring maintenance deferrals, influence system reliability and expected service lives of facilities?

Infrastructure Junction Points and Common-Use Corridors

With increasing coordination of infrastructure planning and rehabilitation, junctions between subsystems become increasingly important. Significant advantages might be achieved through relocation of compatible elements in common-use corridors, within public or private rights-of-way (e.g., power line corridors or streets). Rapid transit on a highway median strip is a frequently cited example that may be extended to a wider range of new and current infrastructure services. Research is needed to assess intermodal linkages and benefits and costs of space allocated to infrastructure. Typical questions for research might include the following examples:

- What would be the life-cycle costs and impacts of consolidating separate systems in common-use underground or elevated corridors?
- What are the merits or disadvantages of alternative strategies for use or preservation of easements associated with obsolete infrastructure elements (e.g., abandoned rail lines, underused highway rights-of-way)?
- What role does infrastructure play in the obsolescence of developed areas (e.g., urban precincts, small cities and towns, and economic regions)?
- How does development intensity influence land requirements for infrastructure?
- Can recreation parks and other environmental infrastructure (e.g., linear parks, wildlife corridors, and green strips) be integrated effectively with other infrastructure?
- Are current infrastructure systems excessively vulnerable to terrorist acts?
- What risk-management strategies will provide effective protection against multiple hazards that may cause interactive disruptions of infrastructure (e.g., water line failures that cut off power supplies, transportation accidents that disrupt telecommunications)?
- How should current systems be modified to facilitate adoption of distributed or decentralized infrastructure technologies (e.g., changes in public buildings to accommodate decentralized power generation)?

Private and Public Interface in Infrastructure

Research is needed into costs and benefits of various management structures and forms of infrastructure ownership. The often ideological discussion of private versus public roles and the relationships among private and public elements of the system hinders careful examination of alternative management methods. Research on this topic could include analyses of historic examples and legal reviews, and comparative studies of different subsystems (e.g., solid waste collection, transportation, and fire protection).

Typical questions for research might include the following examples:

- Can meaningful international comparisons of infrastructure management structures be made?
- How do public or private ownership and management influence rate of adoption of new technology (e.g., cellular communication and highway and street traffic information systems)?

- Do new infrastructure technologies necessarily entail bias toward new land development rather than toward developed areas where retrofit would be required?

STANDARDS, REGULATIONS, AND OTHER EXTERNAL INFLUENCES

Many factors such as current engineering standards and practices, governmental regulations aimed at environmental protection and public safety, general economic conditions, and political forces influence the way infrastructure is developed and used. These factors are external influences on decision making, shaping the options available to designers and operators, public perceptions of infrastructure and its impacts, and the likelihood that assumptions made at each stage of a facility's life cycle will subsequently remain valid.

While such factors thus play a key role in determining infrastructure performance and service life, understanding how they operate is limited. Research is needed to extend this understanding, drawing on basic principles in economics and the social sciences (e.g., multi-attribute utility theory, hedonic pricing, systems modeling, and public opinion research methods), as well as technological forecasting and engineering systems analysis. Payoffs from research in this area include help for infrastructure developers and managers seeking to mitigate adverse environmental, safety and health, social, and economic impacts, and to avoid unexpected public resistance to infrastructure development and operations.

Shifts in Design and Management Objectives

Infrastructure design and management objectives change over time as a result of new technical knowledge, new regulations, or other factors, often as a result of shifts in public values and perceptions. For example, the Americans with Disabilities Act requires retrofitting barrier-free access in all public buildings. Emerging concerns about cancer risks of exposure to electromagnetic radiation may lead to changes in electric-transmission-line design standards. Research to estimate the full benefits and costs of such changes could encompass technical assessments of past and potential future changes and the social and political forces involved in the occurrence of change.

Typical questions for research might include the following examples:

- How susceptible is current infrastructure to obsolescence caused by changes in design objectives?
- Do current regulatory processes use available information effectively to assess life-cycle costs of new regulations and design standards?

- Can rational models be developed for assessing regulatory needs based on variables such as risk, affordability, and quality of environment?
- How have federal, state, and local infrastructure subsidies and regulations influenced urban development patterns?

New Approaches to Siting and Technology Decisions

Decisions about infrastructure siting and applications of technology (e.g., nuclear power) are typically made in a public forum and depend on availability of adequate and credible information. Research is needed to support improved procedures for estimating first-, second-, and lower-order effects of the installation and operation of infrastructure systems and their facilities and for presenting this information in forms usable in the public decision-making process. This research could include a broad range of technologies, such as new simulation modeling, technology assessment, information display procedures, interactive information-query systems, and public voting and joint-decision-support systems.

Typical questions for research might include the following examples:

- What economies in infrastructure development and operations can be achieved by means of effective public education and participation in decision making?
- How can network managers and users gain more effective practical understanding of network operations and management?

NOTES

[1]Another BRB committee, with sponsorship of the U. S. Army Corps of Engineers, is working on a study to consider how such a definition might be developed. That committee's report is scheduled for completion early in 1995.

[2]The term, used by economists to refer to the consequences of opportunities foregone when a decision is made to devote resources to a particular end, is useful for all infrastructure professionals.

[3]The effect that a system's efficiency increases rapidly as more people or businesses are connected to the network.

[4]The effluent from baths, clothes washing, and other activities that do not pose serious health hazards, termed "greywater," is often suitable for landscape irrigation, window washing, or other such uses.

[5]Benchmarking is the measurement of current system performance in terms that provide standards, i.e., "benchmarks," against which future performance may be judged. Research in this topic is also suggested in the context of technology management (Chapter 9).

[6]SCADA technology is increasingly used in the electric-power industry and larger cities' drinking water supply systems to operate larger systems with fewer staff. Research in this area is also addressed with respect to information management (Chapter 5).

MORTON STREET VENT SHAFT, MANHATTAN, NEW YORK
Siting the shaft for the trans-Hudson PATH tubes raised a conflict between purely functional criteria and community interests. In the event local impact took precedence: a park was included with a waters-edge setting. Such situations give rise to questions for research, such as "What economies in infrastructure development can be achieved through effective public education and participation in decision making?"

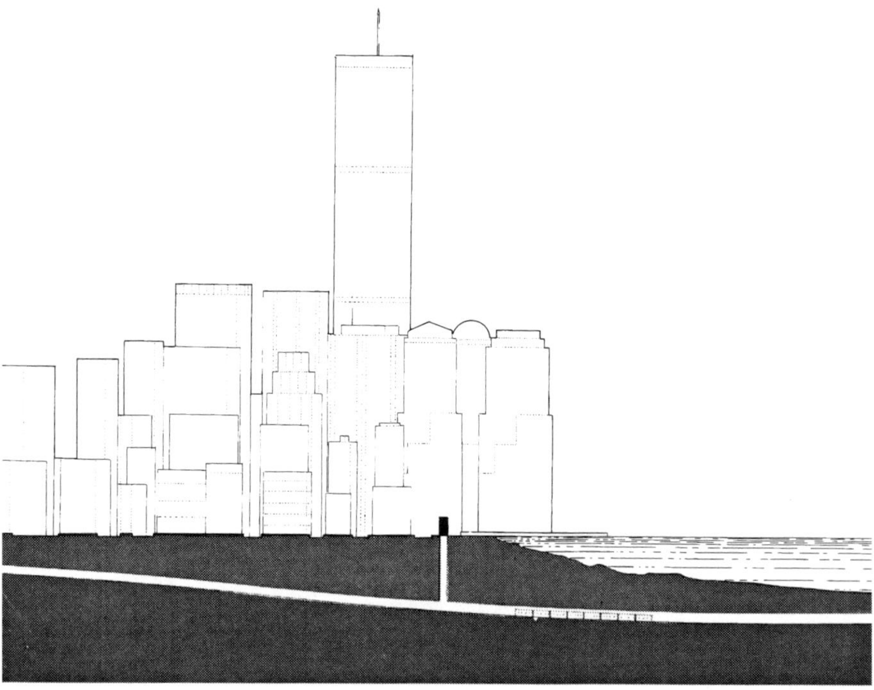

4

ANALYSIS AND DECISION TOOLS

With the introduction of new materials, improved measurement abilities, and expanding environmental concerns, infrastructure professionals find their old analysis methods, planning and design tools, and rules-of-thumb no longer adequate for decision making. Research is needed to develop better tools for assessing the service behavior of infrastructure components, the interactions among components, service problems that may be encountered, and their solutions.

Improved methods for forecasting need, regulatory changes, and societal demands, for assessing impact and risks associated with new and innovative practices, and for modeling system behavior will provide rational, documentable analysis and will support policy decisions. Payoffs will include improved ability to incorporate nontechnical, societal requirements, issues; and benefits into infrastructure planning, design, and operations decision making.

Repair and upgrading decisions are often poorly integrated with either long-term planning or day-to-day management. Constrained resources for planning and condition assessment of physical systems too often do not allow timely, cost-effective decisions regarding infrastructure repair or rehabilitation. Allowing infrastructure systems to deteriorate to the point that replacement becomes the only viable option is simply no longer acceptable. Separation of construction and operations responsibilities among different agencies often aggravates this problem. Research to support operational tools for condition assessment and maintenance management will facilitate planning of systems repair, rehabilitation, or upgrading.

The committee proposes that the NSF should foster research to develop analysis, planning, and design tools that will support integrated infrastructure management. These tools, in many cases applied by professionals operating in areas not well covered by traditional educational programs, must bridge among disciplines. Three major research areas that offer high payoff potential are discussed in this chapter:

1. development of systems models that planners, designers, and managers can use to consider the interactions of infrastructure modes among themselves, with their service environment, and with changing user demands;
2. development of ways to achieve faster integration of new technology into infrastructure design and management practice; and
3. development of improved methods for anticipating consequences of catastrophic events and developing appropriate response strategies.

SYSTEMS MODELS

Few interactive models of infrastructure system components have been developed that can effectively be employed in planning and design settings. While network models for transportation, water supply, and electrical energy transmission are routinely used in planning, these models have limited abilities to address intermodal interactions or related issues such as environmental quality and multiple use of public facilities. Urban development and operations models that could be used at large scales have poor records for accuracy in relation to their costs, and suggest that improvements may lie in sharply reducing costs rather than increasing complexity.

New models of energy delivery systems, for example, would support analysis of the entire process from primary source generation to waste-product disposal. Areas of largest analytical uncertainty include technology improvement forecasts, fuel substitutability, and waste-product disposal, issues that are not easily addressed using most standard analytical tools. In the area of telecommunications, policy analysis methods are needed to support consideration not only of intra-system options but also of linkages among information and data processing.

Computers, information management practices, and sensor technology are enabling "real-time" monitoring of infrastructure conditions and fast management responses (Chapter 5). Infrastructure professionals need tools to take full advantage of these capabilities for improved responsiveness to demand and mitigation of adverse effects of infrastructure deterioration or failure.

Research in this area would deal primarily with development of reliable and cost-effective procedures for forecasting system behaviors and selecting among plan, design, and operating alternatives. Included in this range of research would be efforts to improve methods for demand analysis, particularly with respect to intermodal effects and consequences of uncertainty. Assessment of experience is needed to support modification or replacement of currently used models and methods.

Ex Post Analysis of Planning and Design Methods

Research is needed to review and evaluate experience with infrastructure in service versus assumptions and conclusions on which planning and design decisions were based. Remote-sensing technologies and survey collection of socio-economic data may be required to support such research. Case studies could identify critical points in infrastructure decision making and clarify how decision support tools influence outcomes, giving attention to technical and nontechnical (i.e., societal and political) factors.

Typical questions for research might include the following examples:

- How do experiences with siltation at locks and dams compare with design expectations, and are changes in design methods warranted?
- Can remote-sensing technologies developed for defense and space applications be adapted to infrastructure condition assessment and maintenance management, site assessment, and demand estimation?
- How has infrastructure usage changed with time in ways that were not anticipated in planning and design (e.g., changing patterns of community development, service needs, and substitutions of new services for older ones)?
- Can life-cycle models be developed for predicting system performance as a function of design details for those infrastructure modes that lack such tools?
- Can risk management and environmental pollution-abatement models (particularly for nonpoint sources) be developed to bring concern for these issues into the range of routine planning, design, and operational decision making?

Demand/Capacity Analysis

Infrastructure elements seldom have a clearly defined capacity limitation. Typically, increasing demand leads to increasing usage and degrades performance, which then inhibits demand. Highway traffic congestion is perhaps the clearest example of this effect, but delays in receiving telephone dial tones, flickering electric lights, and variations of water pressure demonstrate its symptoms in other infrastructure modes. A variety of research is needed to improve understanding of the relationship of demand and capacity, develop new tools for analysis, and explore ways to enhance performance of current systems through demand management.

Typical questions for research might include the following examples:

- Are there practical design alternatives for separating segments of demand (e.g., cars and trucks on highways) and thereby improving overall system performance?
- Can ways be found to reduce demand through intermediate processing (e.g., separation and reduction of solid wastes, ramp metering of highway access, and improvements in fiber-optic-system repeater-station technology)?

- Can better models be developed for estimating costs, risks, and reliability effects of setting design and management criteria to meet less-than-peak demands (e.g., post-yield behavior of piping and structural members, queue formation and clearance at toll plazas)?
- What are the short- and long-term costs and benefits of shifting or suppressing peak demands (e.g., delayed access to health-care facilities and flow control on bridges)?

FASTER INTEGRATION OF NEW TECHNOLOGY INTO DESIGN PRACTICE

Designers and constructors too often seem to fail to understand the full range of impacts of new technology, and how to effectively incorporate these impacts into practice. New technology represents unknown risks and impacts that may entail uncertain liability. Research is needed to develop design methods and risk assessment criteria that will allow design, construction, operation, and maintenance practices to readily adapt promising innovations.

Typical questions for research in this area, which may be related to studies in technology management (Chapter 9), might include the following:

- Can improved analytical and design methods be developed for polymeric compounds, ceramics, composites, and other new materials that are particularly susceptible to creep, exhibit time-dependent stiffness variations, rely on toughness to resist failure, or otherwise are poorly suited to analysis with traditional tools?
- Can procedures be developed for rapid estimation of performance limits for new materials, particularly plastics, ceramics, and composites?
- Are changing societal values and priorities likely to warrant significant changes in building codes and design criteria?
- Can more effective systems be developed for rapidly disseminating information about new infrastructure technology to decision makers and the public?

ANTICIPATING CONSEQUENCES OF CATASTROPHIC EVENTS

Recent catastrophic events such as the Loma Prieta and Northridge earthquakes, Hurricane Andrew, and flooding along the Missouri and central Mississippi Rivers can yield valuable information for improving infrastructure design and management practices to respond to rare events and extreme conditions. (See for example, *Practical Lessons from the Loma Prieta Earthquake,* NRC, 1994.) Liquefaction of sand fills, saturation and weakening of water retaining earthwork, and wind uplift on roofs are among the effects poorly addressed in current design guides. Research is needed to analyze such experience and to develop appropriate analysis tools and design and operating responses to reduce future risks.

Research should address ways of assuring reliability of new technologies, such as fiber-optic telecommunication lines, that may be especially sensitive to earthquakes and other catastrophic events. Applications of alternative technologies, such as cellular communications, may be more flexible or resistant to damage but may have higher costs. Construction activities adjacent to infrastructure elements may cause effects similar to catastrophic natural events, and should also be included in such research.

Construction Effects on Lifeline Systems

Disruptions of some elements of infrastructure—such "lifeline systems" as water and electric power supply to critical facilities like fire stations and hospitals—pose especially important risks to public health and safety. Research is needed to improve infrastructure managers' abilities to avoid and respond to such disruptions, especially those caused by construction effects such as excavation-induced ground movements and blasting vibrations.

Typical questions for research might include the following examples:

- What deformations are likely and what are tolerable in fiber-optic cables and conduits subject to differential ground movement?
- Can generalized guidelines be developed for the redundancy needed to manage risk in infrastructure networks likely to be exposed to catastrophic service conditions?
- Are new design procedures needed for retaining structures and man-made fills exposed to earthquake or other catastrophic events?

Emergency Infrastructure Operations Procedures

When catastrophic events occur, ability to maintain infrastructure services often makes a substantial difference in levels of loss and time to recovery. Research is needed to improve procedures for emergency planning and management for infrastructure systems. Susceptibility to terrorist attack is a factor that may be included in this research topic.

Typical questions for research might include the following examples:

- Do risks of loss from terrorist action against key infrastructure elements (e.g., bridges, tunnels, and reservoirs) warrant retrofit strategies to increase protection or reduce loss?
- Are current standards for infrastructure emergency performance assuring acceptable levels of risk?

1989 FIRE IN THE MARINA DISTRICT

COMPUTER SIMULATION OF SAN FRANCISCO WATER SUPPLY SYSTEM

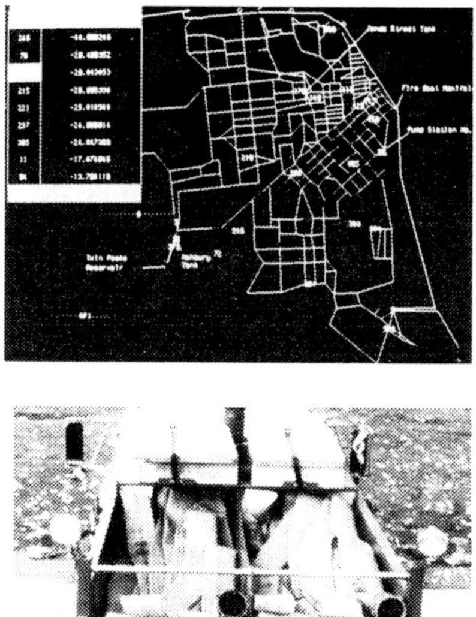

COMPUTER SIMULATION OF EMERGENCY WATER SUPPLY

A computer model of the San Francisco water supply system was developed with support from the National Center for Earthquake Engineering Research and the National Science Foundation. The model, which was implemented at Cornell University, was used to secure public support for system upgrades, including special vehicles which each carry nearly a mile of hosing and above-ground hydrants. The 1989 Loma Prieta earthquake cut all pipeline inflow of water to the Marina District, as predicted by computer simulations. Using the special vehicles, fire was stopped before it could spread to adjacent blocks, thereby saving lives and substantial property loss. Research is needed to improve procedures for emergency planning and management of infrastructure.

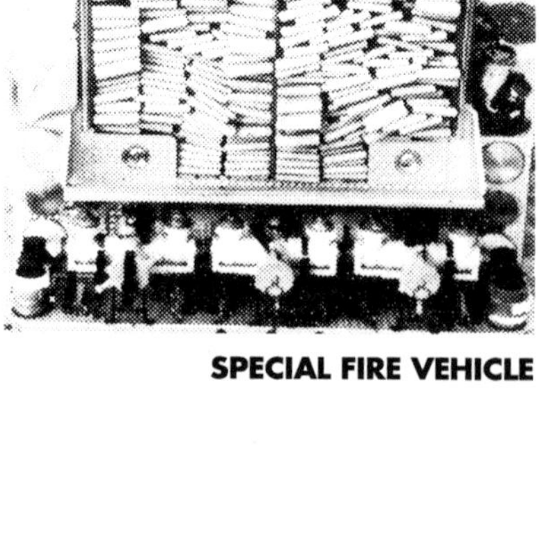

SPECIAL FIRE VEHICLE

5

INFORMATION MANAGEMENT

Infrastructure systems are extensive and complex. Their description includes a substantial accumulation of data that continues to grow as the service lives of facilities progress. Potentially valuable information is sometimes lost or neglected because data are in a form that cannot be accessed easily by decision makers. Rapid and accurate acquisition and storage, processing, and retrieval of information about the system are key to cost-effective management. This information can document current status, simulate future performance of components and interdependent subsystems, and project and evaluate trends in demand and usage.

Rapidly increasing data acquisition, management, and analysis capabilities—associated with advances in measurement, computation, and communications technologies—have made information management a distinct discipline. Research is needed to adapt improved information-management tools to infrastructure development and operation. Particular issues include collection of as-built descriptions of facilities and data on maintenance and rehabilitation that may substantially alter a facility's physical characteristics as well as its operating behavior, over periods of several decades.

The potential payoffs of research include improved confidence in the bases for planning and design decisions, and enhanced operating efficiencies, all due to improved information for decision making. These benefits in turn can improve safety of operation, workforce efficiency, and system reliability.

Research is needed to adapt information-management technologies for infrastructure problems. This research should target fundamental advances in these technologies, to enhance their value in addressing the unique characteristics of infrastructure. Three research areas that offer high payoff potential are discussed in this chapter:

1. adaptation of advanced data acquisition and management methods developed for defense and aerospace, that can collect and maintain integrated and up-to-date descriptions of infrastructures, their performance, and their environments, to make the data accessible for wide application;
2. development of more cost-effective and accurate network analysis methods for characterizing and modeling behavior of infrastructure systems at several geographic scales; and
3. development of tools and information to support professional and public education for more effective management of the investment in infrastructure.

ADVANCED DATA ACQUISITION AND MANAGEMENT METHODS

Infrastructure systems are subject to changing demand and environmental conditions. Daily and seasonal variations in weather as well as more gradual shifts in soil conditions, ground cover, and other characteristics of the region will influence both service loads and operating characteristics of many elements of infrastructure. Remote sensing based on earth-satellite imagery and expert systems for data interpretation that have been developed for defense and agriculture may be adapted for infrastructure development and management in urban regions, but research is needed.

Remote-Satellite Imagery

High-precision data suitable for describing infrastructure location and condition are being acquired continuously by earth satellites. The U.S. Department of Defense, for example, operates a global positioning system with approximately 22 such satellites, and with the purported capability of determining a transportation vehicle's position to within inches. Satellite-collected imagery includes microwave, infrared, and visible-light data that might provide a wealth of information on physical conditions of facilities. However, research is needed to make these data available for infrastructure development and management.

Typical questions for research might include the following examples:

- Will the current resolution of satellite imagery, especially in the visible-light range, support detailed assessment of the physical condition of engineered structures, as well as soil and rock foundation substrata?

• Can systems be developed for rapid acquisition and assessment of structural, soil, and rock conditions following earthquakes, hurricanes, and heavy snows and rainfall, or in advance of potentially hazardous weather conditions?

• How can global positioning systems be developed for control of aircraft, vehicular road traffic, and vessels using harbor and canal facilities?

Improved Use of SCADA[1]

SCADA (systems control and data acquisition) systems have been developed for use in water-supply, natural-gas, liquid-fuels, and other infrastructure systems. SCADA systems use remote sensors and telemetry to collect and transmit data to regional or central control facilities where operational decisions are made. Research is needed to further develop SCADA systems, particularly regarding uses of graphical display, computer algorithms for automated (i.e., "smart") control, and enhanced performance in emergencies.

Typical questions for research might include the following examples:

• Can SCADA be augmented with computer-assisted graphical network modeling for real-time infrastructure system simulation and decision making?

• Can "smart" systems be developed to support emergency system operations, including rapid allocation of "dedicated lines" to enable delivery of critical resources?

• What new technologies are needed to support installation and use of equipment (e.g., computer and radio receiver) in vehicles to receive and process up-to-date traffic information and make adjustments in route plans (e.g., the "intelligent" vehicle).

NETWORK ANALYSIS METHODS

Research is needed to develop improved procedures for infrastructure network representation and simulation. Such research should focus especially on finding ways to better utilize geographical and subsurface geotechnical data in conjunction with data on facility condition and socio-economic bases for demand estimation. These various data are typically collected and maintained on different geographic systems, and algorithms are needed to extrapolate from one system to another (e.g., network links, census zones, and drainage basins).

Aggregation and Disaggregation Methods

Network analysis models must generally be developed at a level of detail appropriate for the questions to be addressed. Too much fine detail consumes excessive computational resources, while having too coarse a network sacrifices accuracy and ability to represent the consequences of alternative plans or operating policies. While substantial advances have been made for moving from one geographic scale of analysis to another, many procedures remain to be developed. Research is needed to enable better integration of operational, condition, and environmental information that influences network performance.

Typical questions for research might include the following examples:

- Can general algorithms be developed for aggregation and disaggregation of multifunctional infrastructure networks in a particular geographic area?
- Can environmental data be represented at several geographical scales without losing critical information?

Intermodal Interactions

One of the most important needs in infrastructure is to manage the interfaces among the various lifeline and utility systems. There is currently no comprehensive means for doing this, although it is technically feasible through computer graphics to simulate the layout and operation of a subsystem (e.g., water supply, electric power, and natural gas). In an urban environment, these systems are interdependent: a gas- or water-main rupture can shut down electrical power, which can then cut off water-pumping capacity and track signaling for rapid transit and street traffic signals. Research is needed to support integrated information systems to deal with these intermodal interactions.

Typical questions for research might include the following examples:

- What data and network modeling capabilities are needed to deal with damaged systems, to represent nonlinear flows, partial system disruption, and time-dependent intermodal damage propagation?
- Can digital video technology be adapted to show time-dependent simulation of multimodal network performance and failure modes?
- Can quick methods be developed to identify and characterize "hot spots" within various utility networks, where the local failure of one component can have severe repercussions for adjacent components of different subsystems?
- Can optical-disk technology be adapted for easy storage and rapid retrieval utility maps and repair records?

EDUCATION FOR INFRASTRUCTURE MANAGEMENT

Many aspects of infrastructure lie underground or in remote locations, hidden from the user's view. Even infrastructure professionals have diffi-

THE FIRE ALARM TELEGRAPH
First constructed in Boston in 1851 by physician William F. Channing and electrical inventor Moses G. Farmer, the fire alarm telegraph created a new urban network. Channing conceived the concept as a sort of "municipal telegraph" that could play a role similar to the human body's nervous system, covering "the surface of the municipal body as thickly with telegraphic signalizing points as the surface of the human body is covered with nervous extremities or papillae. . .". Under the Channing-Farmer plan, Boston was subdivided into fire districts and wires strung between thirty-nine alarm boxes and a central station. The operator would indicate the fire location by energizing a set of bells distributed throughout the city as well as by sending a signal to the alarm boxes. Widely adopted by cities and towns, by 1902 there were 764 systems in the nation. The fire alarm telegraph also facilitated the movement away from volunteer fire companies to more professional organizations.

culty comprehending the complex relationships that underlie performance of geographically extensive facilities with very long service lives, that comprise infrastructure. Research is needed to enhance understanding—by both professionals and the public—of these relationships and the value that infrastructure represents as a public asset, and thereby to improve the overall ability to manage and protect the system.

Such research would explore how information about infrastructure is best presented to enhance access and understanding. Taking advantage of new opportunities for rapid transmission of high volumes of information to homes or offices requires that ways be developed to process and usefully display that information for the recipient.

Using Information Highways

Development of "information highways," generally envisioned as high-capacity, fiber-optic conduits for vast quantities of information, could make available on home or office televisions detailed information about system condition (e.g., congested highway segments, heavy water demands for fires or other emergency situations, and stormwater drainage problems). Research is needed to determine how such capabilities can be used to modify demand to improve performance and more generally instruct the public and technical community on infrastructure issues requiring attention.

Typical questions for research might include:

- How can transmission of emergency-response instructions and infrastructure condition following earthquakes, floods, hurricanes, and tornadoes be made more effective?
- Can education and retraining programs for infrastructure professionals be made more effective through remote learning?
- How can enhancing public awareness of key infrastructure problems at earlier stages in the problem's development help to expand options and improve system management?
- Can video-conferencing or other such tools provide cost-effective improvements in coordination of utility and emergency-response personnel after major accidents and natural disasters?

Uses of Multi-Media

Graphical displays, computerized games, simulations, and multimedia (i.e., pictures, sound, and printed information) are increasingly important tools for decision analysis and general education, enabling presentation of complex information in formats that can be most readily grasped. Research is needed to adapt such tools for use in briefing public officials and other decision makers on key issues and available options for development and management of infrastructure.

Typical questions for research might include:

- What are the most efficient means of presenting technical information to those who may not be expert in the technologies under scrutiny?
- How can interactive presentations, in which decision makers can be directly engaged in exploring "what if" questions, enhance the quality and public acceptance of infrastructure decisions?

NOTE

[1]Research on SCADA is also addressed with respect to system life-cycle management (Chapter 3).

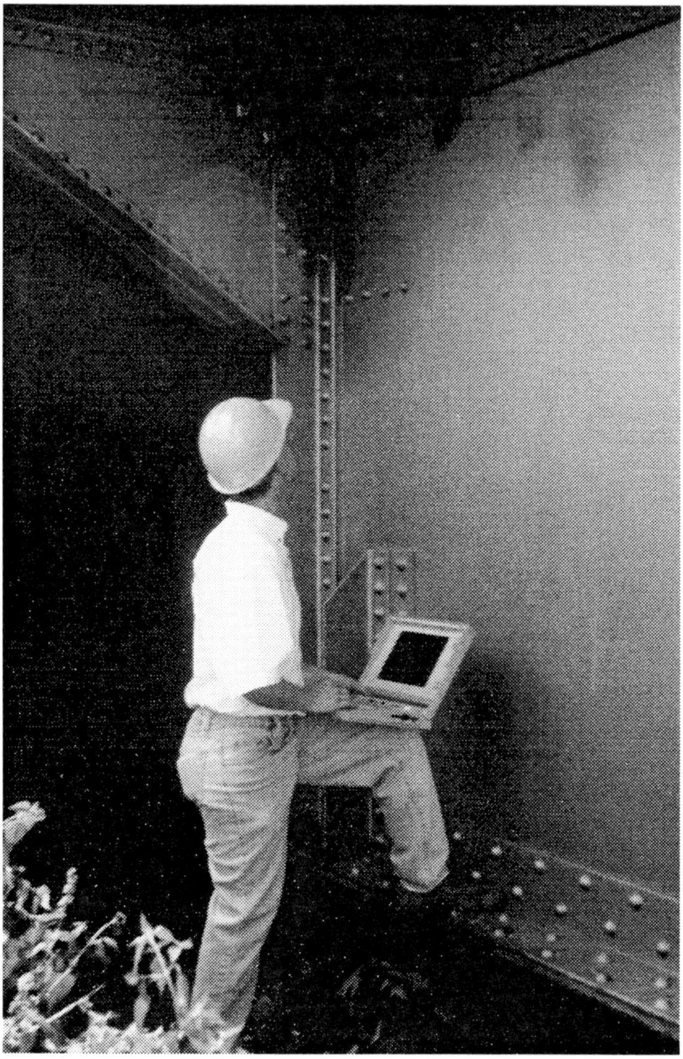

BRIDGE INSPECTION DATA PROCESSING
Computer applications can enhance all aspects of infrastructure management. Here, field inspection of a bridge will be supplemented by expert-system software to help determine whether levels of metal fatigue require special attention. Such systems effectively make available to the field inspector a much broader range of experience than any one person is likely to accumulate in his or her career. Research can yield better methods for characterizing system behavior, monitoring system condition, and anticipating and responding to threats to overall performance.
(Photo courtesy of ATLSS, Lehigh University)

6

CONDITION ASSESSMENT AND MONITORING TECHNOLOGY

Infrastructures normally deteriorate slowly and often in subtle ways that are difficult to observe until substantial damage has occurred. For some facilities the nature and rate of this deterioration are sufficiently well understood to warrant regular inspection and preventive maintenance. More often, the costs of such assessment must be weighed against the prospect of avoiding maintenance and accepting the risk of structural failure and its potential impact on service. Costs of condition assessment and monitoring often appear high because facilities are massive, geographically separated, not readily accessible, or difficult to examine without interrupting service. However, these costs are typically much lower than those incurred when service deteriorates or fails.

Concerns about various components of the infrastructure have traditionally made for a piecemeal approach to research, development, maintenance, and rehabilitation, but resource constraints and subsystem interactions mandate the more global system-wide view that underlies this study. Furthermore, experience has taught infrastructure professionals that environmental and economic as well as technical factors must be considered. Research on condition assessment and monitoring technology will have the greatest payoff if it fosters development and management of infrastructure as a broad, multidimensional service. Three research areas that offer high payoff potential are discussed in this chapter:

1. extension of science and technology for more effective techniques for nondisruptive, nondestructive, monitoring of facility conditions;

2. development of methods for system-wide condition monitoring; and
3. development of better ways to monitor environmental factors and manage by-products or residuals of infrastructure operation.

NONDISRUPTIVE, NONDESTRUCTIVE, CONDITION-MONITORING TECHNIQUES

Nondestructive evaluation of the entire infrastructure is a key element in the effective management to insure maximum benefits to users and minimum costs to owners. Evaluation methods must deal with both surface and subsurface elements: e.g., street and highway and rail networks at grade, in tunnels, and on bridges; intermodal transfer facilities (e.g., ports and airports); pipelines and cable networks; and water supply and wastewater treatment facilities.

Current condition assessments, using both visual and mechanical nondestructive evaluation methods, are meant to provide data for deciding on effective maintenance, rehabilitation, and replacement actions. Research on assessment methods could enhance timeliness and availability of information for decisionmaking. Condition assessment of structures and site characterization are considered in this section.

Structural Assessment

Research on structures is relevant to a wide range of infrastructure. Bridges and electric-power or telecommunication transmission towers are perhaps the most obvious applications, followed closely by institutional buildings. However, the design and management of water and waste containment structures, highway pavements, and tunnels and pipelines have all been substantially improved by developments in such areas as finite-method analysis, characterization of dynamic loading, and stress-strain behavior of complex materials. Much of this work is done by professionals specializing in particular types of structures or materials.

Improved maintenance and rehabilitation of pavements could significantly decrease the cost of goods transport both in terms of truck operating expense and reduction of goods damage from rough roads. The same is true for rail networks since improved maintenance and rehabilitation can prevent damaging and costly derailments. Nondestructive testing is a part of this evaluation process. The SHRP (Strategic Highway Research Program) provided impetus to methods for nondestructive pavement evaluation.[1] However, effort is still needed to assess pavement condition and structural capacity. In addition, improved methods for measuring the pavement profile are needed to minimize pavement damage and optimize packaging of goods as well as to establish roughness criteria for the emerging Intelligent Vehicle-Highway Systems.[2]

The structural response of institutional buildings and bridges to severe loading conditions, such as seismic and hurricane force winds, is not yet fully understood. Designers must rely on empirically derived design methods and codes. Research can enhance knowledge of the behavior of such structures under severe loading, development of damage and failure, and analysis of risk.

Typical questions for research might include the following examples:

- How can accurate indicators of pavement condition and profile be developed and maintained for street and highway pavements in service without disrupting traffic speed and flow?
- Can more accurate and cost-effective methods be found for measuring and monitoring *in situ* characteristics of pavements, that protect the pavement's performance capability (e.g., nondestructive methods)?
- How can structures be effectively instrumented to monitor response to dynamic or transient loading where partial collapse or failure of elements may occur?
- What methodologies can be effectively applied to detect and monitor critical stress changes and damage in steel, concrete, and timber bridges?
- Can adaptive control devices (e.g., self-healing devices) and supporting algorithms be developed to cost-effectively reduce structural failure risks under nonlinear response and large deformations?
- Can "smart" and "intelligent"[3] materials be developed for structural monitoring and control purposes in buildings and other structures subjected to low-intensity repetitive loading?
- Can automated, nondestructive detection, measurement, and evaluation methods be developed for building maintenance and rehabilitation and for sewage collection and water distribution systems?

Site Characterization

Site characterization, an essential part of condition assessment and monitoring technology, deals with procedures to locate and define features within the subsurface environment. For the infrastructure, subsurface environment may be distinguished at two different scales: "near-surface," typically within 5 meters of the ground surface, or "conventional depth," encompassing soil, groundwater, bedrock, and underground structures within the zone of influence associated with particular construction activities.

The near-surface zone contains the pavement, most buried utilities, and relatively shallow underground structures. It is within this zone that the majority of new utility installations and maintenance are carried out.

Because of the crowded nature of urban and suburban neighborhoods, it is highly desirable to identify and locate existing utilities and obstructions without excavation. Avoiding the disruption that accompanies excavation yields great advantages with respect to time, risk exposure, and environmental impact. The effective use of nonintrusive sensing procedures is important for promoting reliable and cost-effective applications of trenchless construction.[4]

Nonintrusive sensing technologies such as electromagnetic methods, magnetometers, acoustics, ground penetrating radar, and infrared detection systems are now used for locating buried pipelines and obstructions. Some of these technologies, such as electromagnetic methods, have been used in practice for a number of years. For example, electromagnetic technology was developed in conjunction with user feedback and has evolved into a variety of commercially available devices. Questions remain, however, regarding measurement accuracy, maximum operative distances and coverage areas, and signal strength from various inductive devices. Research may also provide the bases for other technologies.

Such technologies, developed initially for exploration, may be adaptable to infrastructure condition monitoring and management, especially for underground conduits and pipelines, tunnels, and other buried structures. Remote on-line chemical monitoring of water quality during treatment and distribution and in-service performance of telecommunications equipment (e.g., switches, repeaters, and signal amplifiers) could improve system reliability and economy.

Typical questions for near-surface research might include the following examples:

- How can improvements be made in signal transmission and processing to enhance application of magnetometers and ground-penetrating radar for reliable location of buried utilities?
- Which nonintrusive sensing technologies are most promising for locating subsurface plastic piping, and how can the accuracy of such procedures be enhanced?
- Are there combinations of various sensing technologies which, in aggregate, provide an improved and more accurate detection system?

Conventional-depth site exploration and characterization typically rely on soil borings and soundings. These methods are used for *in situ* soil and rock testing and to recover soil and rock samples for laboratory assessment. Such *in situ* testing devices as cone penetrometers, pressuremeters, dilatometers, and vane-shear equipment, and geophysical methods such as seismic refraction and electrical resistivity are capable of delineating underground features at a relatively small scale and with moderate refinement, but substantial improvements could be made in accuracy and cost-effectiveness. Transfer of technology from medical and other fields offers particular challenge and promise.

Typical questions for conventional-depth research might include the following examples:

- Can seismic tomography (i.e., three-dimensional images created by processing seismic data) be developed for more detailed site characterization?
- Can spectral analysis of surface waves, either generated by special on-site equipment or by background microtremors associated with street traffic or other ambient activities, yield useful information on conventional-depth conditions?
- What geophysical methods, or combinations of methods, are well suited to delineating subsurface strata and constructed facilities, and what degree of resolution and accuracy can be achieved in crowded urban settings?
- Can geophysical methods or penetration devices be applied to characterizing intrusion, concentration, and migration of contaminants in groundwater?

SYSTEM-WIDE CONDITION ASSESSMENT

Component interdependence and the inevitable competition for both monetary and spatial resources make system-wide condition assessment of the infrastructure an important concern, distinct from individual components. Condition monitoring and assessment may be needed continuously or at regularly scheduled intervals throughout the system, but is essential where failure would be catastrophic. The 1992 flooding of freight tunnels in Chicago, which knocked out other systems throughout a multi-block downtown area, illustrated the system-wide effects and monumental costs that can be caused by damage to a single infrastructure element. Research can yield better methods for characterizing system behavior, monitoring system condition, and anticipating and responding to threats to overall performance.

Typical questions for research might include the following examples:

- Can flow monitoring determine location and severity of obstructions, damage, or leakage in water-supply and sewerage networks?
- Can real-time data collection and computer-based simulation be combined effectively for management of infrastructure lifeline systems to improve both service reliability and emergency response strategies?
- How can the degree of risk associated with aging, weakened, and abandoned infrastructures be assessed and evaluated?
- Can protocols, storage and access systems, and financing arrangements be developed for centralized data repositories for complete site profiles (e.g., buried utilities, subsurface conditions, environmental hazards, and hydrologic conditions) in metropolitan areas?

ENVIRONMENTAL FACTORS AND MANAGEMENT OF RESIDUALS

Infrastructure systems and the environment interact in many and often subtle ways. Infrastructure may be the source of contaminants that require monitoring, control, and disposal. Increasingly numerous and stringent environmental regulations have added new constraints to which infrastructure design and operation must respond.

The primary concern addressed in these regulations is the residuals or waste products of infrastructure activities that influence air and water quality, energy consumption, and solid waste management (e.g., construction wastes and roadside rubbish). At the same time, infrastructure plays a role in the management of residuals of other activities, for example when the ash from coal-fired electricity generation processes is used in concrete. Research can yield both better understanding of these interactions of infrastructure and environment and more effective ways to use these interactions to enhance environmental quality while maintaining high levels of service in the infrastructure.

Chemical Grouting

The effect of chemical grouting,[5] commonly used in both foundation construction and waste containment, on groundwater quality must be carefully analyzed and monitored to avoid adverse effects on water supply. The introduction of new grouting materials and procedures has been effective, yet raises grave concerns as to their effects on groundwater quality. Both laboratory and full-scale field studies are necessary to determine the effectiveness and long-term impact of grouting. Typical research might consider whether more effective procedures can be developed for characterizing and monitoring the water-quality influence of grouting, or whether new chemical grouts pose a threat to groundwater safety.

Management of Infrastructure Waste and Residuals

The services that infrastructure provides (e.g., transportation and waste disposal) themselves produce residuals that must be managed. Research is needed to enhance understanding of the processes of waste production and ways to reduce and manage these wastes.

Disposal of residential and commercial wastes in landfills or abandoned mine and quarry excavations poses threats to surface and groundwater quality and hazards related to methane and hydrogen-sulfide emissions. The large areas and heterogeneous compositions of landfills make their management more challenging. Research leading to development of continuous monitoring of process variables and ambient conditions would facilitate process optimization and risk management.

Typical questions for research might include the following examples:

- Can improved techniques be found for monitoring the change in landfill properties (e.g., density, compressibility, and permeability due to biodegradation)?
- What procedures will be most effective for monitoring long-term effects of groundwater seepage in altering landfill constituents and diffusion of contaminants?

Air-pollution monitoring technology has focused primarily on vehicle emissions and pollution concentrations, with relatively little linkage to traffic operation and control. Research could lead to better strategies for traffic control to reduce both emissions and concentrations of vehicular air pollution. A typical research project might consider whether computational models can be developed to link vehicle emissions and traffic flow data, to support metropolitan traffic management.

Urban heat gain in heavily congested areas results in high cooling energy use and may exacerbate problems associated with urban smog. Landscaping using shade trees and light-colored surfaces can lower air temperatures and reduce energy consumption for cooling. Light-colored surfaces stay cool because they typically have a high albedo[6] and reflect solar radiation that would otherwise heat the surface. Using more highly reflective surfaces to increase the albedo of a city would conserve energy and reduce pollution, an alternative that is both economically and environmentally attractive. However, reflections from buildings often cause significant increases in the temperatures of surrounding sites, making the problem of reducing urban heat gain very complex.

Typical questions for research might include the following examples:

- Can meteorological and smog modeling be used to assess the effects on air quality of metropolitan urban and landscape design to control albedo?
- What are the relative merits of conventional dark-colored and more reflective alternative materials for extensive urban surfaces (e.g., roofs and pavements)?

Sewage treatment in metropolitan areas yields substantial volumes of sludge that is typically sent to landfills for disposal. Some progress has been made in the search for alternative uses for this residual material, but many questions remain regarding how to increase the proportions of waste that can be used and whether products manufactured with sewage sludge as a constituent pose particular hazards.[7] Typical research might explore instrumentation, data collection and analysis systems, and other tools needed to support cost-effective, long-term performance monitoring and assessment of paving blocks, vitrified blocks, and other products that incorporate sewage sludge.

NOTES

[1]SHRP was a multi-year program established by federal legislation, following a recommendation by NRC.

[2]IVHS refers to applications of electronic guidance-system and computer technology in highways and vehicles to enable higher system performance.

[3]The terms "smart" or "intelligent" are used in this context to denote materials that provide indicators of their condition without additional instrumentation (e.g., by changing color or emitting electrical signals).

[4]Refer also to Chapter 8 for discussions of trenchless and other underground construction research issues.

[5]Chemical grouting involves injection of low-viscosity material, such as Portland cement or bentonite clay slurry, into porous soil and rock formations to strengthen or significantly reduce the permeability of the formation.

[6]Albedo is a scientific measure of the degree to which energy is reflected rather than absorbed. Absorption of solar energy raises the temperature of highways and roofs to levels much higher than surrounding air temperatures.

[7]Uses of residuals in construction and product development is also a subject for research in the science of materials performance and deterioration (Chapter 7).

PIPE INJECTION WITH ANAEROBIC SEALANT

CYCLIC TEST OF POLYMER SEALANT

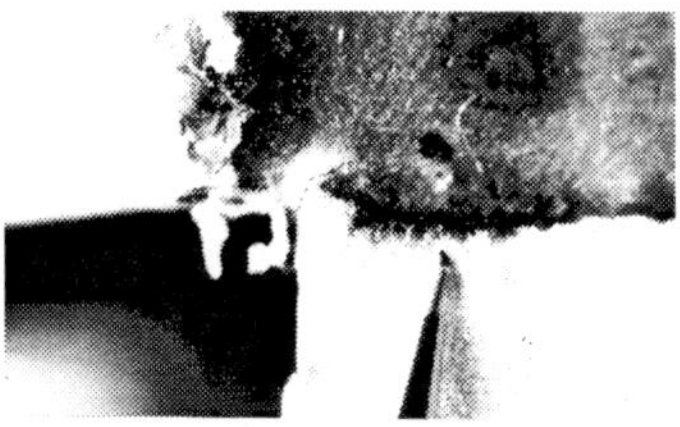

NEW MATERIALS FOR AGING INFRASTRUCTURE

Hundreds of thousands of miles of cast iron mains are used for U.S. water and gas distribution—over 10,000 miles in New York City alone. To improve the performance of these aging systems, new materials—using polyurethanes and anaerobic methacrylates—are being developed by gas utility and chemical companies to seal leaking joints. Because of the scale of U.S. infrastructure, more effective use of materials presents significant opportunities for improved performance and cost savings.

PIPELINES UNDER WALL STREET
New York City, circa 1917

7

SCIENCE OF MATERIALS PERFORMANCE AND DETERIORATION

The abilities of materials scientists and engineers to tailor materials from the atomic scale upwards to achieve desired functional properties have been increasing at rapid rates.[1] The timespan between insight and application is shrinking, with the processes of discovery and development becoming increasingly more interactive.

Materials science and engineering are rooted in the classical disciplines of physics and chemistry. Investigations of structure and composition are focused on the electronic and atomic scales. At the stage of applications in infrastructure, the scale is large: elevated rail and highway structures, long-span bridges, long or large diameter pipelines. Infrastructure material science and engineering must span this range of scales, moving from the clean rooms and other specialized environments of the laboratory to the dirty and highly variable conditions of construction and infrastructure-in-use.

A major challenge of infrastructure research is to promote a productive interaction among material scientists and practicing engineers so that fundamental advances through new material developments can be effectively integrated into practice, yielding more durable and reliable structures and system components. Research activities should enhance communication between scientists and engineers, and stimulate interaction between basic and applied research.

Materials for construction, protection, maintenance, and repair of facilities are basic to all infrastructure. Materials such as Portland cement, steel, and asphalt are used widely and in large volumes. Epoxy resins, glass fibers, aluminum and thermoplastic polymers, and other substances have been less widely used. Nevertheless, because of the scale of the U.S. infrastructure, more effective use of all these materials presents significant opportunities for improved performance and cost savings.

Many infrastructure components experience progressive damage that eventually necessitates major repair or replacement. Micro-cracking occurs in concrete pavements, tunnel linings, bridge structures, and pipes, while fatigue in metals and polymeric materials reduces their reliability. Sometimes this damage proceeds more rapidly than anticipated, due to unexpected usage, severe environmental conditions, or statistical extremes in material variability. Payoffs of infrastructure-oriented research in the science of materials performance and deterioration could include enhanced strength, durability, ease of manufacture and construction, as well as reduced costs and environmental and safety hazards. Two research areas that offer high payoff potential are discussed in this chapter:

1. development or adaptation of high-performance materials for infrastructure; and
2. improved analysis methods for characterizing damage, deterioration, and aging in infrastructures.

HIGH-PERFORMANCE MATERIALS

Because of economic constraints, more cost-effective utilization of existing infrastructure, such as nuclear power plants, roads, bridges, and pipelines, is imperative. In addition, new infrastructure often must be constructed adjacent to or beneath existing facilities that severely limit available space and allowable deformation of structures and soils. Such construction increasingly depends on new and unorthodox materials and composites—for example, high-alloy steels, glass-fiber-reinforced resins and concrete and polymers—that offer high strength, low weight, and durability, that were, until recently, available only in aerospace, weapons, and other high-technology applications.

Polymers

Polymers display a wide range of properties, which make them highly adaptable to the variable conditions and uses that characterize infrastructure. Many polymers have mechanical attributes in the form of high strength, high flexibility, and lightweight. Electrical, thermal, and optical properties make certain classes of polymers especially well suited for specialized applications. The rapid growth and widespread use of high- and medium-density polyethylene (HDPE and MDPE) and polyvinylchloride (PVC) in underground piping networks attest to the importance of such materials. Over 90 percent of all gas distribution piping placed today is composed of polyethylene. Applications on this scale illustrate how effective polymers have proven as substitutes for metals in portions of the infrastructure that once were dominated by steel, cast iron, and copper. Indeed, as reported in a previous study (NRC, 1989c), structural polymers are already in widespread use and account for a major portion of the $100 billion global market for polymers.

Polymers also have been put to good use in infrastructure systems to control water and gas leakage, provide protective coatings, and improve the performance of bearings. Both PVC and HDPE membranes have been applied extensively to restrict water leakage in landfills and tunnel linings. Polyurethanes and epoxies are applied as sealants and protective coatings to a wide range of above-ground and subsurface structures. Methacrylates are used to seal gas piping under anaerobic conditions. Composite polymers are incorporated in the bearing systems of bridge decks and in seismic base-isolation components for building protection.

Typical questions for research might include the following examples:

- What are the characteristics of conductive polymers? How can such materials be used as protective coatings, leakage membranes, and water barriers, which will have the ability to sense and locate imperfections and breaches leading to leakage or exposure?
- How can the strength, load/deflection characteristics, and durability of structural polymers be improved for more frequent application in infrastructure systems? What are the properties of such materials, and how can these properties be specified and used most effectively in design?
- What are the most effective test procedures for accelerated aging of polymeric materials, and how can the associated test results be applied in design?

Geosynthetics

Geosynthetics comprise a class of substances that has evolved rapidly over the last decade, primarily for use in association with soil and rock. The materials have played an increasingly important role in promoting secure landfills, stabilizing roadbeds and embankment foundations, reinforcing slopes, and strengthening waste retention systems. They are used with virtually all forms of drainage control, road construction, landfills, and reinforced soil systems. Their importance with respect to infrastructure derives primarily from their integration with soils to improve the performance of foundations, soil structures, and in-ground drainage and retention systems. Geosynthetic materials perform several major functions, such as separation of different grain sizes, reinforcement of soil, filtration and drainage in subsurface fluid control, groundwater control, and as barriers to fluid movement in and around underground structures. Geosynthetics may be manufactured as textiles or fabrics, grids, nets, and membranes, and are composed of polymers, rubbers, fiberglass, and other material constituents.

Typical questions for research might include the following examples:

- What stress relaxation behavior can be expected from different geosynthetics and how can it be characterized for analysis and design?
- What are the failure mechanisms of geosynthetics in earth retention systems and reinforced slopes? How can small- and large-scale experiments be directed most effectively to clarify the fundamental nature of failure and soil-structure interaction of geosynthetically reinforced walls and slopes?
- Are there effective ways of *in situ* spraying or spreading geosynthetic materials, and what are the durability and other performance characteristics of materials thus applied?
- What are the tolerable levels of deformation and disturbance associated with geosynthetic membranes, reinforcing systems, and composites of two or more geosynthetic products?

Other High-Performance Material Applications

Opportunities for high-performance materials in infrastructure extend well beyond structural applications, warranting research on a very broad range of questions. High operating-temperature superconductors could improve electric-power transmission efficiencies and possibly enable development of effective magnetic-levitation transport systems. New optical-fiber materials might enable power transmission and improved resistance to adverse operating environments. New patching and fill materials could improve pavement maintenance efficiency. Fiber-reinforced polymer-based composite materials with high strength-to-weight ratios and corrosion resistance could replace conventional materials in bridges and increase the bridges' load-bearing capacities. Chemical or biological additives could give concrete, earth, and rockfill structures (e.g., dikes and embankments) abilities to "heal" when damaged by seismic or other unusual loads. Coatings could signal when strain or damage to structural elements has progressed to levels warranting maintenance.

CHARACTERIZATION OF DAMAGE, DETERIORATION, AND AGING

Those responsible for infrastructure design and management need mathematical models and other analytical tools to select facility design characteristics, and operating and maintenance strategies to ensure cost-

PIPE JACKING BENEATH RAILWAY

PIPELINE CROSSING OF HIGHWAY

PIPELINES CROSSING TRANSPORTATION ARTERIES

High-pressure gas and liquid fuel pipeline crossings of highways and railroads have been viewed as inherently hazardous, and significant interest in this issue has been expressed by the gas, petroleum, highway, and railroad industries. Research supported by the Gas Research Institute at Cornell University was undertaken to perform three-dimensional stress and deformation analyses of pipeline crossings, field test instrumented high-pressure pipelines beneath heavily loaded railway facilities, and develop standards for pipeline crossing design and installation practice. The development of new procedures and technology acceptable to many different industries required an intensely coordinated effort. The research has resulted in a new design methodology adopted by the gas industry, and embodied in the standards promulgated by the American Railway Engineering Association and the American Petroleum Institute. Research could support development of new standards as well as immediate improvements in infrastructure performance.

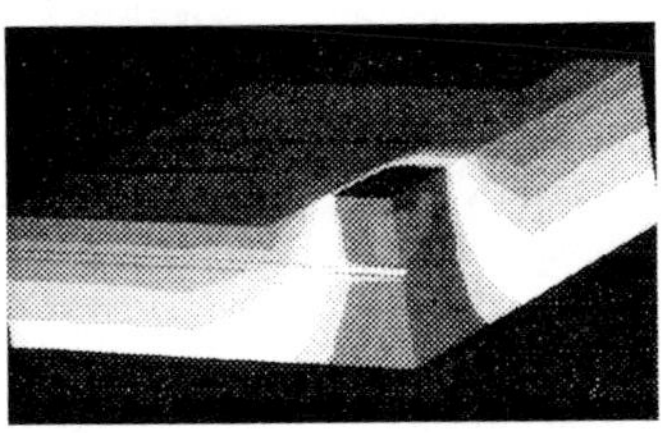

COMPUTER GRAPHICS STRESS ANALYSIS OF PIPLINE CROSSING

effective performance. These analytical procedures must accommodate material behavior such as crack propagation, visco-elastic and plastic response to loads, dilation, and other nonlinear elastic behavior. Such mechanisms depend on loading, temperature, and other environmental conditions. In pavements, pipes, and large building or bridge structures, discontinuities at joints and in foundation materials must be considered.

Improved constitutive relationships for analysis procedures, as well as better defined damage and failure criteria, will permit the more effective utilization of the various materials in infrastructure. This in turn will significantly extend the life and reduce costs associated with damage caused by increasing traffic volume and loads on pavements. The same is true for assessment of existing structures such as buildings and bridges in seismically active areas.

Limit States and Failure Criteria

Better understanding is needed of the mechanisms and conditions that lead to failure of materials in infrastructures. Crack initiation and propagation in conventional materials, such as asphalt and Portland cement concrete, as well as newer plastics and composites, are difficult to observe, model, and predict. Reliable failure criteria could be developed, using stress/strain invariants, for composite materials subjected to multi-axial stress over a wide range of temperatures and loading frequencies (e.g., nuclear-waste containment facilities, fuel tanks, pipelines in environmentally sensitive sites).

Time-Dependent Deformation and Strength

Better understanding is also needed of the long-term behavior of materials that exhibit nonlinear elastic, visco-elastic, and plastic response to loading, such as asphalt concrete, plastics, and other polymeric materials. The effects of temperature and aging on these and more traditional civil engineering materials (e.g., steel and Portland cement concrete) are complex and have yet to be well represented by analytical models.

Typical questions for research might include the following examples:

- Can computational algorithms be developed to enable more effective three-dimensional finite-element idealizations to be used in the analysis and design of infrastructure components (e.g., representing dynamic response of concrete pavements including the effects of discontinuities such as joints and voids, and permanent deformations in asphalt-concrete pavements)?
- Can reliable models be developed for analysis of corrosion fatigue in bridge structures and underground steel and cast-iron pipes?

Cost-Effectiveness Assessment

Materials used in infrastructure must perform over long periods of time. Development of new materials is hampered by the need to simulate long-term service conditions or to collect and analyze data over long periods. Research to find cost-effective methods for materials performance testing could yield substantial payoffs.[2]

A particularly difficult set of questions has to do with materials that use waste products (residuals) from other infrastructure activities. Sewage sludge and fly ash (produced by burning coal for electric-power generation), in particular, can contain heavy metals or other constituents that may eventually leach out to contaminate water supplies or otherwise pose environmental and health hazards. Research could yield better methods for assuring long-term stability of waste-incorporating construction materials.

Typical questions for research might include the following examples:

- Can expert-systems software be developed for infrastructure materials evaluation (e.g., categorizing weld quality and inspection data for bridges and power-plant systems)?
- Can rapid-proofing methods be developed for determining stability and other performance characteristics of materials incorporating waste products (e.g., sewage sludge and fly ash)?

NOTES

[1]For further discussions of developments in materials sciences, see for example, *Materials Science and Engineering in the 1990s, Maintaining Competitiveness in the Age of Materials,* published in 1989 by the National Academy Press.

[2]Research in this topic area is related to condition assessment and long-term monitoring (Chapter 6) intended to support infrastructure management.

JACKED SEWER PIPE ON STATEN ISLAND, NEW YORK

The Oakwood Beach collector included 7,000 feet of 63" O.D. jacked pipe made of a new combination of woven fiber-glass, polyester resin and silica sand. This is a Swiss innovation, manufactured by a computer-controlled spinning process. It offers high yield strength, 12 to 16 ksi, lightweight, easy handling, low friction to facilitate jacking and increased hydraulic capacity. At an 85-foot depth, the jacking rate reached 122 feet in a 12-hour shift, using a mole with crunching ability to handle the glacial soil. Such examples illustrate the value of answering such research questions as these: How can the strength, load/deflection characteristics and durability of structural polymers be improved for more frequent application in infrastructure systems? What are the properties of such materials, and how can these properties be specified and used most effectively in design?

8

CONSTRUCTION EQUIPMENT AND PROCEDURES

Infrastructure systems typically require large-scale construction, which involves high-cost, capital-intensive financing, and long time to completion. The work often is carried out in densely populated, highly developed urban areas or environmentally sensitive locations. Research is needed to enhance construction productivity, minimize hazards and environmental impact, and reduce costs.

HIGH-PERFORMANCE CONSTRUCTION TECHNIQUES

Effective construction technology and management can reduce the time required to build or repair infrastructure, and thus reduce costs, minimize site disruptions, and improve quality and safety. Off-site fabrication, "just-in-time" delivery of materials and labor to the site, reusable formwork, and climbing cranes are examples of performance-enhancing construction techniques introduced in recent years. While many construction innovations are project-specific, research on the broader issues of enhancing construction productivity, for example with computer-aided tools and equipment or new construction materials, could yield substantial returns to the industry and to infrastructure performance.

Improved Information Exchange

Improved construction efficiency often depends on better utilization of the substantial capital invested in equipment and materials. More effective information exchange among on-site operations, fabricators and suppliers, and the central design offices, for example through constructibility assessments and short lead-time scheduling, improves efficiency. Research to improve information and its management in construction could produce further significant improvements.[1]

Typical questions for research might include the following examples:

- What tools and procedures could enhance communication and information transfer of as-built construction data between the design office and construction site?
- Can more efficient and accurate construction site documentation improve equipment utilization and control and product quality?
- How can three-dimensional spatial data-management systems and simulations be most effectively used for construction site management?
- Can electronic data interchange reduce costs and improve efficiencies in the business of construction, i.e., transactions among owners, designers, constructors, and vendors?
- What must be done to develop or adapt site-positioning technologies, such as satellite global positioning systems (GPS) and laser- and radio frequency-based systems, for construction site use?

Off-Site Pre-Fabrication

One of the most important recent advances in infrastructure construction, particularly in structural systems, has been in the use of pre-cast or pre-fabricated units mass-produced at a specialized central facility and delivered "as-needed" to the construction site. Research could further enhance the efficiencies and quality improvements of off-site component fabrication, for example by improving construction tolerances and product durability. Research directed at enabling transport of fabricated construction elements from shop to site could also yield substantial benefits.

Resource Scheduling

Effective resource utilization (e.g., skilled labor, specialized materials, advanced equipment, time, and funds) is crucial to construction efficiency. Available resource-scheduling techniques, typically based on critical-path methods and other linear mathematical methods for project activity scheduling, are often inadequate for the multiple-objective, multiple-constraint complexity of large projects. Research could yield improved methods for characterization of project constraints, optimization algorithms, and cost-effective systems for making advanced management methods accessible to project personnel.

Typical questions for research might include the following examples:

- Can the design or installation of a system or component be optimized with respect to financial and other resources?
- Can the physical and resource constraints be balanced to improve the overall cost-effectiveness of the project and completed system?
- How might design of specific infrastructure components or systems better reflect the resource constraints operating in a particular geographical or physical environment?

CONSTRUCTION WASTE DISPOSAL

Infrastructure construction, maintenance, and rehabilitation inevitably produce excavated earth materials (termed "spoil"), nonrecyclable wastes, and other debris. Replacement of old infrastructure produces volumes of demolition debris. Disposal or other disposition of such wastes is often complicated by concerns that the materials may be contaminated by petroleum products, heavy metals, asbestos, or other hazardous substances. Excavations to repair pipes and other buried infrastructure frequently uncover unexpected wastes from long-discontinued industrial activities. The scale of these problems generally falls short of the cases dealt with in the Environmental Protection Agency's Superfund cleanup program, but the experiences are similar.

Federal agencies such as the Corps of Engineers and Environmental Protection Agency have sought to address elements of the problem, but further research is needed to make systematic improvements in construction waste reduction and management. Methods that combine efficient disposal, constructive reuse, and effective recycling would relieve the pressure on dwindling available disposal sites adjacent to urban centers. An extension of this philosophy might encourage the development of more environmentally sensitive facilities.

Dredge Spoil

Past studies, sponsored primarily by the Corps of Engineers, have sought to improve methods for disposal of dredge spoil, and a number of full-scale disposal sites have been established. Containment islands, such as Hart-Miller in Baltimore Harbor, and salt-marsh construction in Chesapeake Bay could point toward more environmentally sensitive means to deal with recurring dredge-spoil problems. However, careful field evaluation of such schemes is needed to characterize their impact and support development of planning and design guidelines for use elsewhere.

Typical questions for research might include the following examples:

- What are fill consolidation rates and related effluent characteristics for containment area design?
- What are the technical and economic comparisons of various forms of spoil containment and salt-marsh construction?
- Could drying procedures enable the use of dredge spoil as soil cover for sanitary landfills, lightweight construction fill, or agricultural soil nutrient?

Characterization and Assessment of Contaminated Sites

The accumulated impact of decades of industrial activity has increased the uncertainty in infrastructure activities, regarding the environmental consequences of excavation and construction in areas where toxic or hazardous materials might be encountered. Characterizing and treating these contaminated sites becomes an unanticipated and very costly addition to the work of infrastructure renewal and development.

Research is needed to support better methods for determining the extent and severity of contaminants, for characterizing the threat they pose in soil and groundwater, and for assessing the consequences of alternative abatement strategies. Research is also needed to devise better strategies for decontamination or effectively immobilizing contaminants *in situ*. Better bases are needed for determining appropriate levels of site investigation and remediation, and for monitoring long-term results of remediation efforts.

Typical questions for research might include the following examples:

- Can risk assessment models be developed to reduce variability and public controversy regarding estimates of contamination and response to such assessments?
- Can remote sensing and nonintrusive on-site reconnaissance and measurement methods be developed to improve characterization of contaminated sites?
- Can remote data-acquisition systems be utilized to monitor long-term performance of treatment and remediation?

Dry Construction Waste

Even when sites are not thought to be particularly contaminated, the management of urban soils excavated during infrastructure construction and improvement often requires comprehensive chemical assessment to satisfy stringent governmental solid- and hazardous-waste laws and regulations. Typically, chemical constituents of concern include volatile organic compounds, semi-volatile organic compounds (including polyaromatic hydrocarbons), metals, and petroleum hydrocarbons. These constituents have entered the soil through such routes as combustion of leaded gasoline (now completely phased out), waste and deterioration from lead-based paints (not generally available now), applications of pesticides and herbicides, leakage and spillage, and residues from industrial activities. The presence of such contamination limits the options for reuse or disposal of these construction wastes.

Soil sampling and testing programs must balance the needs for environmental protection with the realities of demanding construction schedules. Research is needed to facilitate rapid screening for hazard and reduce laboratory costs and response times. Better methods are needed for biological or chemical treatment of contaminated soils to permit their reuse.

Typical questions for research might include the following examples:

- Can new test procedures be found for rapid, cost-effective sampling and testing or *in situ* evaluation of soil chemical composition?
- Can soil admixtures, injection grouting, or other means be developed for immobilizing contaminant leakage and effectively sealing areas surrounding buried tanks and pipelines?
- Can cost-effective biological or other methods be found to extract and concentrate soil contaminants in order to facilitate their removal?

UNDERGROUND CONSTRUCTION

A major share of infrastructure construction and rehabilitation occurs below ground or deals with underground structures. Many infrastructure facilities now located above ground would be placed below the surface if costs and safety hazards were not so high. Research to facilitate underground construction could yield substantial environmental and economic benefits, particularly in densely developed urban areas.

Automated Tunneling

Robotic control systems have been, as yet, infrequently utilized in U.S. underground construction. There is tremendous potential for their contribution to safety, efficiency, and economy. Research is needed to develop more efficient mechanized tunneling systems, better methods for investigation and characterization of subsurface conditions to match machine features to soil and rock conditions, and improved modeling of excavation, tunnel support, and ground response to determine support requirements and optimal construction procedures.

Typical questions for research might include:

- What kinds of automated control systems are best suited to tunnel boring machines (TBMs), for both hard- and soft-ground tunnels?
- How can robotics be adapted most effectively to TBMs, particularly for such tasks as mechanized shotcreting, continuous casting of concrete tunnel lining, and automated erection of segmented tunnel linings?

Trenchless Technology

Developments in trenchless technology—for installation, renovation, and replacement of underground utility systems without open-cut construction—has been rapid and extensive, and international competition for markets is keen. The benefits of this technology in urban applications include reduced disruption of street traffic and adjacent businesses, longer service life of street pavement, improved safety for construction personnel, and ground movement and vibration hazards to nearby structures. In wetlands and ecological reserve areas, trenchless construction can avoid disrupting natural systems. Problems of construction spoil are reduced or eliminated.

These substantial benefits have motivated proliferation of methods such as pipe jacking, microtunneling, auger boring, pipe ramming, directional drilling, directional fluid jet cutting, percussive tools, rod pushers, and horizontal slurry drilling. *In situ* renovation procedures for infrastructures include pipe insertions, sprayable seals, structural repair, slip lining, and a variety of polymer lining installations. These various methods have relied, in turn, on advances in drilling technologies and adaptation of microelectronics for guidance and control systems. The field's broad range gives rise to similarly broad opportunities for beneficial research.

Typical questions for research might include:

- Can reliable analytical relationships be developed to link-jacking mechanisms, soil and groundwater conditions, and construction and service loads on pipelines and conduits that are suitable for use by designers selecting pipe materials, dimensions, and installation procedures?
- Can trenchless technologies be used for more cost-effective and safe treatment of contaminated sites?
- Can reliable analytical methods be developed for estimating magnitudes and patterns of ground deformation likely to occur for different trenchless installation methods and different sizes of installed conduit, particularly with regard to volumetric expansion associated with insertion of new or larger diameter piping and conduits?
- How may the economic benefits of reduced business and traffic disruption, pavement damage, and public hazard be most effectively evaluated in order to compare trenchless with alternative construction methods for specific projects?

Hazards Mitigation

Risks of fire, explosion, and other hazards to worker safety in underground construction are high in comparison to other types of construction. Research is needed to develop better methods for assessing, managing, and mitigating these risks.

Typical questions for research might include:

- Can better methods be found for exploration and monitoring of underground hazards such as explosive or flammable materials (e.g., methane deposits), for hazard mitigation (e.g., gas-flow deflection or prevention), and for hazard management within the workspace (e.g., nonflammable materials, fire-suppression procedures, explosion-proof equipment)?
- Can new methods be developed to prevent migration of hazardous liquids into work areas, such as by ground freezing, use of compressed air, well-pumping barriers, cutoff procedures, impervious linings, or membranes?

Construction Effects on Adjacent Facilities

Excavation in soil and rock always disrupts the *in situ* conditions of equilibrium so that adjustments in the form of ground deformations will take place, even though structural support is installed to promote overall excavation stability. In urban and suburban environments, excavations are often undertaken close to buildings and utilities which will be influenced by the ground deformations that accompany the excavation and support process. Moreover, construction often involves the generation of potentially damaging vibrations from blasting, pile driving, or operation of heavy equipment. Accordingly, the permanent and transient ground deformations caused by construction are of critical importance with respect to cost and feasibility of infrastructure projects.

In some cases, vibrations generated by rail traffic can be transmitted through the ground into overlying structures, causing noise that can seriously impair the use of facilities which depend on a relatively quiet acoustic environment. This noise, which is referred to as re-radiated noise, tends to be heard in basements and properties with concrete floors. The recognition of the phenomenon can be very important when planning and designing for underground transit systems in congested urban settings.

Typical questions for research might include the following:

- What are the most appropriate site-exploration methods and analytical models for characterizing soft soil sites, particularly those in highly deformable clays and silts, with emphasis on predicting permanent ground movements in response to deep excavation and construction activities?

• What are the appropriate soil-structure interaction models to account for high-rise building and underground facility response to excavation-induced ground deformation, and can such models be validated by thorough field instrumentation at actual construction sites?

• How does frequency affect the response of various structures to vibrations from blasting and heavy construction, and how should such effects be measured and reflected in construction specifications?

• What are the most reliable and effective means for evaluating the potential for re-radiated noise, and how can new construction be implemented to dampen such effects or to shield existing structures from vibration?

CONSTRUCTION SAFETY

Safety for the neighbors as well as workers on infrastructure construction and rehabilitation activities is a crucial concern, for work in congested areas, often in proximity to vulnerable or potentially hazardous structures, involving heavy or specialized equipment and long hours of work. Research can enhance construction safety by supporting development of ways to reduce human exposure to hazards and levels of injury and damage if accidents occur. Robotics, automated guidance and control of heavy equipment, and ergonomic design are researchable topics from which benefits could be substantial.

Typical questions for research might include the following examples:

• How can hand-held and operator-controlled construction equipment be designed for more productive use and increased safety with respect to accidents, unsafe environments (e.g., dust or noxious fumes), and the hazards of continued repetitive motion?

• What kind of automatic sensing and control systems can be adapted for heavy construction equipment to reduce the risk of exposing and penetrating hazardous structures, such as high-pressure gas and liquid-fuel pipelines, and contaminated soils?

• Can cost-effective robotic systems be developed for inspection and construction at sites having potentially toxic chemicals, flammable or toxic gases, and high risk settings, such as elevated structures and underwater environments?

REHABILITATION AND RETROFIT

Infrastructure rehabilitation and retrofit can cause major disruptions in the functions of a community. Methods to mitigate these problems, such as repair of pavements and replacement of the linings in water pipes, are being developed, but major improvements in rehabilitation methods can still be made.

For instance, new technologies could improve significantly the safety in the work zone as well as minimizing both disruption and community costs.

The key characteristics of rehabilitation and retrofit activities are that major portions of existing systems remain in place, and efforts to repair or replace significant components must be performed *in situ* and must be compatible with elements retained. For instance, the improvement of a water system may involve replacement of pumps or addition of storage tanks at higher elevations, thereby creating greater pressure in supply mains and distribution pipes, which may then fail. Replacement or repair of the pipe sections that failed may likewise induce failure at other places in the system, creating a cycle of repair, breakdown, and repair.

Several of the previously mentioned research niche areas obviously apply to rehabilitation and retrofit, particularly life-cycle management, condition assessment and monitoring, and new materials. However, certain other research areas are specifically connected to infrastructure *in situ* repair, and these can offer significant cost savings in both immediate application as well as through their long-term impact on the planning and practice of rehabilitation and retrofit.

System Isolation

To repair existing infrastructure systems *in situ*, segments of the systems must be isolated. This isolation must be conducted through physical segregation as well as in functions of service performance. A criterion for this isolation is that a segment of the system must be able to be shut off from the system as a whole without causing total system shutdown. Elements that influence the degree of potential isolation for any segment include the size of the segment and redundancy of other elements for service functions, as well as the speed with which work can be performed on the isolated segment.

Some important research questions may include models for effective short- and long-term system isolation, and the selection of appropriate technologies (such as quickly applied remedial materials).

Typical questions for research might include:

- How can a series of rehabilitation activities on an infrastructure system be modeled to decrease the probability of total system shutdown or failure and to minimize system disruption?
- How can temporary redundant systems be used to improve system performance during rehabilitation or retrofit?
- What are some types of mechanisms or components that can temporarily isolate a segment of a system and be easily withdrawn after repair or retrofit?

Access to Degraded Segments

The *in situ* repair and retrofit of infrastructure systems usually involves components to which access is difficult. The specific element which has degraded may underlie layers of other systems (such as a failed structural member within a building) or in other regions which are difficult to reach (such as the geomembrane in a landfill). The costs of dismantling the system to get at the degraded element may be extremely high, but failing to repair the segment may induce additional stresses in the system that can cause more serious failure.

Research could build better understanding of the effects of gaining access to degraded segments. Topics in this area could complement activities mentioned earlier in underground construction.

Typical questions for research might include:

- What are effects of gaining access to degraded segments on adjoining infrastructure systems or on neighboring segments?
- What are the performance criteria necessary for localized and nonintrusive repair and rehabilitation methods, such as the expected life of repair and ability to withstand expected loads?
- How may systems explicitly incorporate access for maintenance and repair into their design and construction?

DECOMMISSIONING

Fluctuating demographics and societal demands have awakened many municipalities to the need to decommission portions of existing infrastructure, or even to close down complete systems. In addition, when severe natural disasters occur, choices must be made on which destroyed or damaged segments will be repaired by order of their priority. Unfortunately, in many disasters, the costs of repairing all damaged elements may be beyond reasonable ranges to replace. For example, the Loma Prieta earthquake destroyed several segments of the highway system in the San Francisco area, including the much publicized and tragic collapse of an elevated interstate highway structure in Oakland. When deciding which segments would be rebuilt with scarce state and federal funds, government agencies decided that the overpass should be completely demolished and not replaced. Other similar choices have been made for the decommissioning of school buildings as the school-age population in a community diminishes, and for water reservoirs as small communities join regional water authorities.

Research in this area could provide immediately applicable insights to agencies contemplating system contraction and decommissioning. It could also provide significant long-term benefits from the improved effective use of infrastructure systems, encouraging the decommissioning (either temporary or permanent) of unused infrastructure, while preserving flexibility to meet future demands.

Temporary Facilities

As the population in a specific region changes, the demands on infrastructure also change significantly. A region with many small children may require a large school system and plentiful public transportation, while a region with an older population may need more handicapped-accessible public buildings and transportation modes. Some of these changes may be best met with facilities that are not designed to be permanent additions to the capital investment of a region, but are rather marshalled to meet the demands as they occur.

The concept of temporary facilities is to minimize the cost of the facilities' construction and maintenance for abbreviated design lives, such as for only 10 or 20 years. Research can be conducted on the attributes of less costly materials for these temporary structures, as well as the design of systems that improve the efficiency of service operations while minimizing maintenance and repair costs.

Typical questions for research might include:

- What are the attributes of temporary facilities that have a curtailed design life, such as the exclusion of expansion capabilities and the use of specific materials?
- What are the construction methods and procedures that can influence the projected design life of temporary facilities?
- How can the design of temporary facilities best accommodate overflow activities from permanent facilities?

Network Devolution

Older urban and suburban areas sometimes find that losses of residents and certain economic activities leave large areas served by infrastructures for which demand no longer exists at the same levels. Agencies responsible for these systems don't have the resources to maintain excess capacity, and often lack the tools to reduce the scale of the subsystem.

Research can explore the issues of infrastructure decommissioning. System elements may be removed from service entirely or their service levels may be reduced, an equivalent of the management strategy of "downsizing." Some elements may be taken out of regular service but maintained for use if unusual needs arise (e.g., during droughts or following earthquakes). Such issues may also be addressed as questions for research on systems life-cycle management (Chapter 3).

Typical questions for research might include the following examples:

- What materials are most conducive to decommissioning, either through lack of maintenance (should the facility be mothballed) or through immediate reuse or recycling?
- What construction equipment, connections, methods, and materials could facilitate the decommissioning of infrastructure systems, for example by increasing ease of disassembly?
- How may the scale of certain infrastructure systems be decreased without reducing the efficiency of adjoining or connected systems?
- What are the acceptable ranges of "overcapacity" for infrastructure systems, and how might the costs for this extra capacity be minimized? Where is this maintenance minimization, rather than decommissioning, appropriate?

PROCUREMENT AND MANAGEMENT PRACTICES

The U.S. construction industry is composed of a relatively few large firms and many smaller businesses that operate in limited geographic areas and technical specialties. While larger firms often utilize sophisticated management procedures comparable with other leading industries, the majority of firms have limited access to such procedures. Further, the industry depends largely on management skills that are not widely applicable in other industries. Thus, research is warranted to improve management practices in infrastructure construction.

Increased efficiency and lower cost in these industries, which are largely tied to public service, imply better service and economy for the public. Management improvements for infrastructure construction can serve as an example and can improve practices throughout the construction industry.

Contracting Practices

Disputes leading to litigation between parties involved in infrastructure construction, as in all civil construction, have led to an adversarial climate that can interfere with legitimate business activities and ultimately increase costs for infrastructure owners and users. The nature of the contractual relationship in infrastructure projects, the assignment of risk and responsibility, and methods of dispute arbitration deserve some priority in research.

Typical questions for research might include:

- Do joint venture agreements between prime contractors and material suppliers affect total job costs?
- Can more cost-effective and equitable risk-apportionment methods be developed for construction and for the completed facility (e.g., con-

struction bonding, workmens' compensation, wrap-up insurance, and designers' warranty)?

- How effective are alternative procedures for contract dispute avoidance and resolution, such as mediation, arbitration, dispute review boards, and partnering concepts?

Project Management Tools

Apart from avoidance and adjudication of disputes and risks, there are many opportunities for improved management practices assisted by computer and data-handling techniques.[2] Research is needed to support methods for providing detailed technical information on-site, such as shop drawings, and for monitoring of quantitative measures of construction project productivity on site and at major off-site fabrication locations. Such systems would in turn enable research into decision rules for scheduling and procurement contingency planning and response strategies.

NOTES

[1]Research in this area may overlap activities discussed in Chapter 5, particularly with regard to advanced data-acquisition methods.

[2]Research in this area overlaps and extends topics discussed regarding advanced data-acquisition and network-analysis methods (Chapter 5) and high-performance construction techniques.

CABLE RAILWAY CONSTRUCTION, NEW YORK, 1891

Introduced in San Francisco in 1873, cablecars were the first mechanical means of propelling streetcars to gain wide acceptance in American cities. They employed a stationary steam engine powering an endless steel cable in an underground conduit. A grip on the car engaged the cable to move cars along rails at an average speed of 12 miles per hour, about twice that of the horsecar. Cable railways were especially attractive in large dense cities because trailers attached to a grip car gave the system high carrying capacity. By 1890 some 225 miles of track had been laid in several cities. However, the systems were very capital intensive and subject to frequent breakdowns. Successful construction, 1888, of an electrically powered streetcar line, in Richmond, Virginia, marked the beginning of a rapid displacement of both cable and horse-drawn systems. By 1902, there were over 22,000 miles of electric streetcar lines in the nation. The heritage of the cablecar remains in some cities, in the form of the large concrete and steel-cable conduits that today hinder street and utility maintenance. Research is needed to provide better understanding of the ways in which new infrastructure technology can be introduced compatibly with existing systems.

9

TECHNOLOGY MANAGEMENT

Technology management links engineering, basic sciences, and management practices to enhance the likelihood that new technology will be developed and successfully incorporated into practice. The field includes technological change, R&D management, technology transfer, and the institutional environments that encourage productivity-enhancing new technology. For infrastructure, which operates within the context of a city or region, this means studies of such matters as inducements and barriers to innovation, public perceptions of technology, government policies that influence private R&D, and distributions of responsibility among public agencies and private enterprise. Research payoffs in this area could include improved productivity of the investment made by the NSF and others who fund research, reduced barriers to infrastructure innovation, and ultimately more rapid improvement in infrastructure performance.

These payoffs will be realized primarily over the longer term, but the current deterioration of many elements of the national infrastructure system and the increasing public attention given to this deterioration make such research more urgent. Hence, the committee recommends that this research should be given a prominent place in the NSF's infrastructure programs. Four major research areas that offer high payoff potential are discussed in this chapter:

1. development of improved analysis methods and management tools for characterizing and achieving high system performance;
2. exploration of technologies in other fields for adaptation to infrastructure applications;

3. development of better understanding of the institutional barriers to infrastructure innovation and how those barriers may be reduced; and
4. development of better understanding of the process by which research leads to infrastructure innovation.

ACHIEVING HIGH PERFORMANCE

Infrastructure is expected to provide a range of services to a diverse mix of users, efficiently, safely, and reliably, for long periods and under varied conditions. The nature of these services has changed in recent years, as new issues have occupied the public's attention, such as the processing and disposal of medical wastes, the retroactive disposal of toxic chemical and nuclear wastes, the reclamation of industrial disposal sites, and the emergency response necessitated by natural disasters or large-scale infrastructure failures. Such new needs are generally not well defined and are seemingly not being effectively met. Research is needed to develop more comprehensive statements of performance needs that are presented to stimulate new ways of providing these services.

Potential payoffs for this research are substantial: reduced damage and loss of life from natural and man-made disasters such as hurricanes, earthquakes, floods, and terrorist attacks; improved flexibility in dealing with environmental impacts of human activities, especially under emergency or other unusual conditions such as drought or industrial mishap; and improved allocation of public investment in infrastructure, reflecting the tradeoffs to be made among diverse design and management objectives.

Defining and Measuring Performance

Research is needed to develop criteria and measures of infrastructure performance that can be used for direct comparison of diverse technological alternatives. For example, it is very difficult to compare directly the long-term merits of investments in transport versus those in water supply, or use of wood versus steel for bridge structures, because of the wide range of factors to be considered. These criteria and measures will necessarily reflect the concerns of several government agencies and private interests, and must be accepted at all levels of the decision-making process to have an impact.[1]

Typical questions for research might include the following examples:

- How can local and national interests and priorities be measured, presented, and balanced in setting infrastructure performance criteria?
- What is the most effective use of system-operations data for performance benchmarking,[2] and what role might public-access performance databases play in infrastructure system management?

Incorporating Externalities

Design and management of infrastructure involves dealing with many externalities[3] such as air and water pollution emissions, neighborhood disruption, obstruction of views, and historic value of structures and neighborhoods. Current practices often neglect externalities or defer their consideration to later stages of decision making. For example, the preparation of environmental impact statements (EIS), mandated by law for many infrastructure construction projects, is generally performed independently of the conceptual and detailed facility design. Research is needed to provide better methods for measuring externalities and internalizing these factors (i.e., incorporating them thoroughly into design and management decision making).

Typical questions for research might include the following examples:

- How should air pollution and leachates be valued in making location and design decisions about hazardous and municipal solid-waste treatment systems?
- What role can public education play in shifting demand or willingness to pay for infrastructure services (e.g., through influence on lifestyles or acceptance of technological risk)?
- How can the full cost of product packaging be most effectively measured and reflected in pricing policy?
- How should historic values of infrastructure facilities and the surrounding areas be measured in undertaking infrastructure repair and replacement in historic urban precincts?
- What are the bases for judging infrastructure facility capacity (e.g., with respect to crowding and congestion, time delay, and availability of service)?

Emergency Procedures

Urban emergencies have opened questions regarding how well prepared current infrastructure systems may be to respond to disruptions or other sudden changes in service demands. For example, during the evacuation of New York's World Trade Center following the 1993 bombing incident, internal communications systems were disabled, and local cable television connections provided the only link to people stranded in the buildings. Burst water mains in the early 1990s have disrupted transit and street traffic, power supplies, and communications in several East Coast cities. Storms in the nation's mid-section and earthquakes in the West have been similarly or even more disruptive. Research is needed to develop better algorithms and operating procedures for detecting, assessing, and responding to infrastructure emergencies, particularly with regard to modal interdependencies. Typical questions for research might include the exploration of opportunities for continuous multimodal monitoring and control systems for urban infrastructure, for example with imbedded sensors, cellular or wired communications, and high-speed data processing.

TECHNOLOGY ADAPTATION TO INFRASTRUCTURE

New technologies are emerging in many fields (e.g., medicine, computing, and consumer electronics) that could be adapted to infrastructure. While some large corporations undertake reconnaissance of emerging technologies to identify product development opportunities, relatively little such work is done for public works. The evaluation of new technologies for infrastructure applications must encompass a broad range of concerns for complementary changes that may be needed for successful adaptation.

TESTING TO FAILURE
Sometimes disasters yield research opportunities. This length of the Cypress Street viaduct, in Oakland, California, remained apparently undamaged following the 1989 Loma Prieta earthquake. To learn more about the causes of structural failures during the earthquake and methods that might be used to retrofit other structures to better withstand future earthquakes, researchers conducted low-amplitude forced-vibration test and high-amplitude static tests on the structure. A final series of tests was carried to levels causing structural deformations and severe damage. (Photo courtesy of Bechtel Corporation, Karl Wiedner, photographer)

For example, development of successful electric-powered highway vehicles will require not only new battery technology, but also systems for routine and emergency recharging of vehicles away from their normal home locations. Such complementary needs could discourage development of a promising new technology.

Research is needed to support development of analytical methods for screening emerging technologies for infrastructure applications, estimating the broad costs and benefits of their adaptation, and developing feasible public policy and strategies for encouraging beneficial adaptations. The payoffs of such research would be realized in longer-term improvement of public health and safety and infrastructure effectiveness.

Technology Compatibility Assessment

Research is needed to provide better understanding of the ways in which new infrastructure technology can be introduced compatibly with existing systems, so that transitions to higher performance may be made without substantial disruptions of existing service areas. While some modes evolve more easily through the rapid spread of small component changes (e.g., materials science leading to change in semiconductors, leading in turn to improved communications), for others the process is more difficult and disruptive (e.g., construction of a new transit system). Research in this area could identify opportunities for significant evolutionary improvement in economic efficiency and functional effectiveness of the system overall, and develop principles for optimal introductions of new infrastructure technology.

Analysis of Technology Markets

Better models and methods to assess the market potential of new infrastructure technologies would be useful in assessing the merits of proposed public investment programs. Infrastructure's high public accountability and dependence on a political budget-making process shape both the way criteria for investment are defined and applied and the scope of the market for new products and services. Market potential studies typically developed by private-sector firms, based on future profit potential, cannot be easily adapted to the public decision process. Research in this area could develop the bases for alternative procedures for assessing market potential and presenting that assessment effectively within the public decision-making context, for example by seeking to define protocols and database systems for public-sector infrastructure technology assessments. Transfers of industrial hydraulic systems for water-resources applications, new fuel cycles for municipal energy supplies, and genetic engineering for hazardous- and municipal-waste cleanup applications are among the topics the committee discussed. New systems for district utility management (e.g., heating and cooling, water recycling, or on-site waste processing for high-density urban areas), leading perhaps to development of "intelligent" districts,[4] is another area of opportunity.

INSTITUTIONAL OBSTACLES TO INNOVATION

Relationships among the various parties involved in infrastructure development and management are often important to how technology is used. For example, the traditional design-bid-build process for infrastructure, with construction bid on a unit-price or fixed-cost basis, can deter technological innovation by removing incentives to innovate. Some observers propose that other procurement methods and contractual arrangements (e.g., design-build, build-own-transfer, and cost-plus-fee construction) are more conducive to infrastructure innovation. Similar claims are made regarding the distribution of ownership and management control between private and public sectors. Research could identify the relative costs, risks, and benefits of nontraditional procurement arrangements.

Such research might explore how environmental quality standards and the enforcement agencies influence infrastructure decision making. Other studies could assess the influence of government and private procurement processes on incentives and obstacles to developers of new technology, and what role ownership structures (e.g., public utility or toll authority versus government department) play in determining willingness to adopt promising new infrastructure technology.

The primary payoffs of research in this area would be improved cost-effectiveness and speed in application of new infrastructure technologies. For example, significantly more-stringent water quality requirements may make current water purification technologies obsolete by raising operating costs to levels that would justify new investment if alternative technology were available. Understanding the scale of these higher costs, when and how they must be paid, and by whom, could provide insight into how research investment, risk-management methods, and system procurements could foster more efficient treatment technologies.

Criteria and Standards

Better understanding of the impacts of government-imposed criteria and standards on infrastructure design and operations is needed. New standards meant to modify narrowly defined infrastructure performance requirements can have much broader effects on related processes and

NEW MATERIALS, NEW FORMS
Higher strength materials and computer-based analysis methods have spurred wider use of cable-staied bridge designs. Elegant structures such as this highway bridge between Huntington, West Virginia and Proctorville, Ohio, are gaining public attention for their aesthetic beauty as well as their structural efficiency. (Photo courtesy of the National Endowment for the Arts, Presidential Design Awards program)

institutions. For example, air-quality regulations currently have decisive influence on transportation operations in many regions. Research could support development of new standards designed to encourage long-term innovation as well as immediate improvements in infrastructure performance. Such research is needed particularly in the management of drinking-water and waste-water quality, air-pollution emissions, and public health effects of infrastructure operations (e.g., electromagnetic radiation from electric-power transmission and telecommunications).

Impact of Procurement Methods

The infrastructure procurement process often is unnecessarily restrictive, effectively excluding new technologies from consideration. Overly detailed and specific lists of requirements, functions, characteristics, or attributes obscure key underlying functions or performance desired. Such restrictiveness arises in trying to reduce uncertainty by controlling process, when methods for measuring performance of the product are lacking. Research in this area could enhance ways that technological risk is measured and managed, as well as the allocation of financial risks of introducing new technologies. Such research could draw on results of research into methods for condition assessment and monitoring (Chapter 6) and education of infrastructure professionals and the public (Chapter 5).

Performance/Cost Trade-Offs Under Uncertainty

More effective analytical models are needed to support evaluation of the trade-offs between performance obtained and likely lifetime costs of infrastructure. The traditional dependence on discounted cash-flow analysis can limit decision makers' abilities to deal with intergroup and intergenerational trade-offs. Information on the relationships between prices and demand for infrastructure services are lacking as well, limiting decision makers' abilities to assess, for example, how increased water rates may suppress consumption, leading in turn to revenue deficits that curtail long-term performance improvement programs. Research could explore hedonic pricing,[5] benefit-cost assessment models for infrastructure-operations scenario analysis, and more effective ways to present benefit and cost information for public decision making.

RESEARCH-TO-INNOVATION PROCESS

The process by which research produces new technology that is subsequently transferred into practice determines how effective R&D spending can be in yielding infrastructure improvement. Research is needed to make this process more effective.

Typical questions for research might include:

- What is the impact on productivity of distributed government support of infrastructure research (e.g., distinct local, regional, state, and federal responsibilities, distributed among separate energy, transportation, or water resources agencies) versus more concentrated management typical of many European countries (e.g., a single national ministry of construction and local authorities)?
- What organizational models for collaboration between educational institutions and local governments are most effective in encouraging research spending that leads to effective innovation?
- Do management programs that focus on organizational performance (e.g., Total Quality Management, management by objectives) have significant impact on rates of infrastructure technological innovation?
- How can an assessment be made of the likelihood that a particular infrastructure management organization will be successful in adapting and applying new technology to achieve improved system performance?

NOTES

[1]The Building Research Board is conducting a study sponsored by the U.S. Army Corps of Engineers on measuring and enhancing infrastructure performance. The report of this study is planned to be published in early 1995.

[2]Benchmarking, the measurement of current system performance in terms that provide standards against which future performance may be judged, is also discussed in the context of system life-cycle management (Chapter 3).

[3]The term is used by economists to refer to product characteristics not incorporated directly into the measures of price and quantity that describe the balance between demand and supply.

[4]Architects and engineers have adopted the term "intelligent" to refer to buildings that incorporate advanced communication and controls for management of their electric and heating and ventilation systems.

[5] Hedonic pricing is a statistical technique used to infer market values people might be willing to pay for goods and services not easily traded on an open market.

INFRASTRUCTURE IN THE LAB
Research on old infrastructure can provide new design information. Here, riveted railway bridge girders that have seen 50 years of service are tested in the laboratory to determine accumulated damage and help researchers develop tests and mathematical models for predicting the remaining service life of old structures.
(Photo courtesy of ATLSS, Lehigh University)

10

RESEARCH LEADING TO INFRASTRUCTURE IMPROVEMENT

Chapters 3 through 9 have presented the committee's selection of topics for infrastructure research that warrant high priority in the coming decade. Many more topics could be suggested and may warrant research effort. However, the topics included in this agenda comprise a broad scope for researchers and their sponsors, and research resources are inevitably limited.

The committee therefore limited its recommendations to the broad, cross-cutting niches discussed here. Because the boundaries among these infrastructure research niche areas are difficult to define, overlap or duplication among specific research topics may occur within the broad scope of the committee's agenda. Because similar topics can be stated from several perspectives, each possibly leading to fruitful results, some overlap and duplication may be a useful characteristic of a robust research agenda. But it should not become excessive and wasteful. Monitoring of progress is needed.

The committee did not estimate explicitly the reasonable or appropriate cost of research projects that might be developed within this broad scope. Explicit estimates of cost must be based on the specific technical approaches and resources to be applied to each study. Sometimes, initial research results will indicate that resources should be applied differently or that a new approach is needed. Again, monitoring of progress is needed, along with mechanisms for feeding information from evaluation back into the direction of future research.

If infrastructure research is to be effective within this context, there must be a continuing commitment over a period of years. Committee members asserted that the strength of this commitment is even more important than total level of funding in determining research outcomes. The medium-term outlook (i.e., ten to twenty years into the future) that the committee adopted in developing its infrastructure research agenda should apply to program development as well.

As the committee noted early in its study, NSF spending has traditionally been allocated and administered primarily along disciplinary lines, rather than in the cross-cutting patterns that infrastructure warrants. The traditional pattern matches the structure of academic institutions that are the NSF's primary grant recipients. The NSF Directorate for Engineering deals largely with academic staffs in schools of engineering; the younger Division of Social, Behavioral, and Economic Research works with schools of economics and social sciences; and other directorates deal similarly with particular disciplinary fields.

The committee also noted, however, that special programs have from time to time been established to encourage collaboration across academic disciplinary boundaries and to address needs not easily placed within traditional organizational structures. In recent years, the NSF has sponsored creation of research centers focused on such topics as earthquake engineering (at the State University of New York at Buffalo), Portland cement technology (based at Northwestern University), and large-scale structures (at Lehigh University).

These centers typically bring together faculty and students from several parts of the university—or even from several universities and outside institutions[1]—to work on projects managed under the umbrella of the center's administrative structure. Typically there is also a physical center of activity with offices, equipment, and meeting areas that provide a base of operations and sense of identity for the researchers and the research area.

While their creation and management often pose substantial challenges within the traditional disciplinary organization of a university, such centers offer advantages of bringing together a critical mass of research activity that begins to produce results greater than might be expected of the parts taken separately. Such famous centers as Thomas Edison's Menlo Park, New Jersey laboratory, the Bell Telephone Laboratory, and Princeton University's Institute for Advanced Studies[2] are frequently cited as examples of highly productive concentrations of research talent and activity. Other newer research centers have demonstrated success at universities throughout the country.

However, the development and management of infrastructure are largely a local matter. While there are common needs and concerns at the national level, the local conditions and demands that infrastructure must serve vary substantially from place to place, influenced by socio-economic conditions, local political relationships, climate, topography, and a variety of other factors. Centers, which concentrate activity and focus on particular topics, will have difficulty responding effectively to the broad diversity of needs in a comprehensive research agenda. The traditionally widespread and curiosity-driven work of individual researchers is better matched to this broad diversity than are the focused activities of centers.

The committee suggests that both traditional single-researcher efforts and focused centers have a place in infrastructure research programs that grow from this agenda. A program that includes a balanced mix of both types of activity, drawing on research resources and responding to research needs around the nation, is most likely to yield solid payoffs of infrastructure improvement. The research may be based at academic institutions, but could as well draw on the resources of government laboratories now being directed toward commercial activity and civilian concerns.[3] This NSF-funded cross-cutting infrastructure research could augment activities at centers established under other programs, such as the 13 University Transportation Centers administered by the Department of Transportation or the NSF's own Engineering Research Centers (ERC).

Regardless of the institutional setting, the research should be undertaken as a partnership of researchers and research users. In particular, municipal and state governments should be participants in the development and management of infrastructure research programs, to assure both that the research reflects problems, and operating conditions actually encountered in U.S. infrastructure systems and that results can be put quickly into practice. Inclusion of private-sector partners (i.e., utility companies, construction companies, and manufacturers) should be encouraged as well. However, financial contribution of all such participants, while highly desirable and often required in other centers programs, should not be a condition for NSF support of a new cross-cutting infrastructure research center. Such a requirement can be a strong incentive to focus research on topics that are closer to commercial development than is the intent of this agenda. Nevertheless, the committee recommends that all NSF-sponsored infrastructure research should be guided by the contributions to be made to practical improvement of the nation's infrastructure, with substantive input from public agencies and industry.

Because the range of research disciplines encompassed in this cross-cutting agenda is broad, the committee recommends that a single, unified program announcement should be issued to invite proposals. This announcement should span all areas of infrastructure research funded by the NSF, and all seven niche areas recommended here.

Such a broad announcement will not match the scope of any current single program or directorate within the NSF, but rather bridges several operating units. Some adjustment in NSF organization and procedures may be needed to relax constraining influences of traditional disciplinary relationships and points of view. However, the NSF's ongoing internal studies to develop CIS programs suggest to the committee that such change will not be particularly disruptive and may already be under way.[4]

Can broad programs of infrastructure research be justified in economic terms? As described in Chapter 2, infrastructure R&D spending has declined substantially in recent years. Committee members pointed out that the nation's private sector routinely expects that financial returns on assets should be 3 to 7 percent annually or more. If the nation's infrastructure, with a value probably exceeding $3 trillion, yields a similar return, the system's aggregate contribution to the nation's economy would be between $90 and $210 billion annually, equivalent to approximately 2 to 4 percent of GNP (gross national product).[5] In addition, infrastructure needs are global, and new infrastructure technology can have high export potential.

If NSF-sponsored research can improve the productivity of the nation's infrastructure by only 1 percent, the benefits would amount to perhaps $1 billion to $2 billion annually for years into the future. But productivity improvements are not the only justification for infrastructure research. Research results will help to conserve and extend the productive life of existing infrastructure assets, and will preempt the failures of infrastructure that, while rare, have such high nonmonetary costs for a community.

The conduct of the research will contribute to the education and training of a new generation of infrastructure professionals. These new professionals will enter their disciplines with a functional appreciation of the multidisciplinary nature of infrastructure and its impacts on the economy, the environment, and society. New teamwork among traditional disciplines will be fostered as well.

Most importantly, new knowledge and technology resulting from this cross-cutting infrastructure research program will ultimately improve the quality of life throughout the nation. By global commercialization and transfers of technology, these benefits can spread to other countries as well.

These many benefits represent a high return to be gained from new investments in infrastructure research, and increased investments may be justified. However, realizing these benefits through infrastructure innovation is achievable only if research results are ultimately put into practice. While support of undirected research that can lead to serendipitous results should certainly continue, priority should be given to research that can plausibly be linked to practical infrastructure improvement. Imagining these links is analogous to preparing a marketing plan for new products nearing readiness for commercial release. The committee has taken a first step in imagining the research topics and improvements to be gained, but it is up to researchers and users of the results to achieve real improvements in infrastructure performance.

President John F. Kennedy and his brothers adopted the words of playwright George Bernard Shaw: "Some men see things as they are and say 'Why?' I dream of things that never were, and say, 'Why not?'" Infrastructure research should be an effort to dream of improvements and find ways to make them happen. That is the aim of the committee, and should shape the NSF's role in supporting infrastructure research.

NOTES

[1]For example, the Portland Cement Association and the National Institute for Standards and Technology participate in the Center for Science and Technology of Advanced Cement-Based Materials, based at Northwestern University.

[2]Such notables as Albert Einstein and John von Neumann have been based at this center.

[3]These institutions in some cases already work closely together, for example, the Construction Engineering Research Labs and the University of Illinois, the Advanced Physics Lab and Johns Hopkins University, the Oak Ridge National Laboratories and the University of Tennessee, and the Forest Products Laboratory and the University of Wisconsin.

[4]The committee was informed by NSF staff of consideration being given to the establishment of innovative management structures, such as "virtual directorates," a term adapted from the "virtual reality" of computer jargon, referring to temporary or informal management units that may not match the organization's formal structure. The committee understands that implementation of its recommended program involves attention by the NSF to many details. The committee believes the NSF's prior experience should provide a good basis for successful program management.

[5]The Bureau of Economic Analysis, U.S. Department of Commerce, reported the nation's 1990 GNP was $5,465.1 billion. GNP is the market value of all goods and services bought and used during the year.

REFERENCES

Blake, N. M. 1956. Water for the Cities: A History of the Urban Water Supply Problem in the United States. Maxwell School Series III. Syracuse, New York: Syracuse University Press.

BRB (Building Research Board). 1986. Construction Productivity. Washington, D.C.: National Academy Press.

BRB. 1988. Building for Tomorrow: Global Enterprise and the U.S. Construction Industry. Washington, D.C.: National Academy Press.

CERF (Civil Engineering Research Foundation). 1991a. Setting a National Research Agenda for the Civil Engineering Profession. 1,2 (August). Washington, D.C.

CERF. 1991b. Transferring Research into Practice: Lessons from Japan's Construction Industry. Washington, D.C.: Civil Engineering Research Foundation.

CERF. 1993a. Federal Public Works Infrastructure R&D: A New Perspective. Report Number 93-EF1003. Washington, D.C.: Civil Engineering Research Foundation.

CERF. 1993b. High-Performance Construction Materials and Systems: An Essential Program for America and Its Infrastructure—Executive Report. Report Number 93-N5011.E. Washington, D.C.: Civil Engineering Research Foundation.

CERF. 1993c. A Nationwide Survey of Civil Engineering-Related R&D. Report 93-5006. Washington, D.C.: Civil Engineering Research Foundation.

CIS Task Committee. 1993. Civil Engineering Systems Research: A Self-Study of the NSF Role. Prepared for Engineering Strategic Planning Committee, Washington, D.C.: National Science Foundation (unpublished, internal document).

Cohen, L. R., and R. G. Noll. 1992. Research and Development, in Setting Domestic Priorities. H. J. Aaron and C. L. Schultz, eds. Washington, D.C.: The Brookings Institution.

Dibner, D. and A. Lemer. 1992. The Role of Government Agencies in Fostering New Technology and Innovation in Building. Washington, D.C.: National Academy Press.

DOC. (U.S. Department of Commerce). 1991. Statistical Abstract of the United States: 1991. Eleventh edition. Washington, D.C.: U.S. Bureau of the Census.

ENR (Engineering News Record). April 6, 1992. 37–40.

ENR magazine, Washington Observer. October 18, 1993. 7.

Grant, A. and A. Lemer, editors. 1993. In Our Own Backyard: Principles for Improving the Nation's Infrastructure. Washington, D.C.: National Academy Press.

Ibbs, C. W. and D. Echeverry. 1988. New Construction Technologies for Rebuilding the Nation's Infrastructure in Cities and Their Vital Systems: Infrastructure Past, Present, and Future. J. H. Ausubel and R. Herman, eds. Washington, D.C.: National Academy Press.

NCPWI (National Council on Public Works Improvement). 1988. Fragile Foundations: A Report on America's Public Works. Washington, D.C.: U.S. Government Printing Office.

NRC (National Research Council). 1984. Committee on National Urban Policy. Perspectives on Urban Infrastructure. R. Hanson, ed. Washington, D.C.: National Academy Press.

NRC. 1985. Technological Alternatives for Urban Infrastructure. J. P. Eberhard and A. B. Bernstein, eds. Building Research Board. Washington, D.C.: National Academy Press.

NRC. 1987. Infrastructure for the 21st Century: Framework for a Research Agenda. Committee on Infrastructure Innovation. Washington, D.C.: National Academy Press.

NRC. 1989a. EPRI (Electric Power Research Institute) Research and Development Program, Electric Power Research Institute. Energy Engineering Board (EEB). Committee to review the management of the Gas Research Institute. Washington D.C.: National Academy Press.

NRC. 1989b. A Review of the Management of the Gas Research Institute. Energy Engineering Board (EEB). Committee to Review the Gas Research Institute's Research, Development, and Demonstration Program. Washington, D.C: National Academy Press.

NRC. 1989c. Materials Science and Engineering in the 1990s, Maintaining Competitiveness in the Age of Materials. National Materials Advisory Board (NMAB) and Board on Physics and Astronomy (CPSMA). Washington D.C.: National Academy Press.

NRC. 1994. Practical Lessons from the Loma Prieta Earthquake. Geotechnical Board. Committee on Fracture Characterization and Fluid Flow. Washington, D.C.: National Academy Press.

NSF (National Science Foundation). 1992a. Civil Infrastructure Systems Research: A Self-Study of the NSF Role. CIS Task Committee for the ENG Strategic Planning Committee. Washington, D.C.: National Science Foundation.

NSF. 1992b. National Patterns of R&D Resources: 1992. NSF 92-330. Washington, D.C.: National Science Foundation.

NSF. 1993. Civil Infrastructure Systems Research: Strategic Issues. Washington, D.C.: National Science Foundation.

Nye, D. 1990. Electrifying America: Social Meaning of New Technology, 1880–1940. Cambridge, Massachusetts: MIT Press.

OFR (Office of the Federal Register). The United States Government Manual 1988/1989. Washington, D.C.: National Archives and Records Administration.

OTA (Office of Technology Assessment). 1987. Washington, D.C.: Government Printing Office.

OTA. U.S. Congress, Office of Technology Assessment. 1990. Rebuilding the Foundations: State and Local Public Works Financing and Management. Washington, D.C.: U.S. Government Printing Office.

OTA. 1991. Delivering the Goods: Public Works Technologies, Management, and Financing. Washington, D.C.: Government Printing Office.

TRB (Transportation Research Board). 1984. America's Highways; Accelerating the Search for Innovation. Washington, D.C.: TRB.

ACRONYMS

APWA	American Public Works Association
ASCE	American Society of Civil Engineers
AWWA	American Water Works Association
BRB	Building Research Board
CERF	Civil Engineering Research Foundation
CERL	Construction Engineering Research Laboratory
CIS	Civil Infrastructure Systems
DOC	Department of Commerce
EIS	Environmental Impact Statements
EPRI	Electric Power Research Institute
ERC	Engineering Research Centers
GEOB	Geotechnical Board
GIS	Geographic Information Systems
GNP	Gross National Product
GPS	Global Positioning Systems
GRI	Gas Research Institute
NAE	National Academy of Engineering
NCPWI	National Council on Public Works Improvement
NIMBY	Not in My Back Yard
NIST	National Institute of Standards and Technology
NRC	National Research Council
NSF	National Science Foundation
OTA	Office of Technology Assessment
R&D	Research and development
SCADA	Supervisory Control and Data Acquisition Technology
SHRP	Strategic Highway Research Program
TBM	Tunnel boring machine
TRB	Transportation Research Board

A

BIOGRAPHICAL SKETCHES OF COMMITTEE MEMBERS AND STAFF

JAMES P. GOULD, Sc.D. (Chairman) is a partner with Mueser Rutledge Consulting Engineers. He specializes in evaluations of prototype performance, application of soil and rock properties to foundation design and engineering geology. He earned a B.S.C.E. from the University of Washington, an M.S.C.E. from the Massachusetts Institute of Technology, and a Sc.D. from Harvard University. He is an Honorary Member of the American Society of Civil Engineers, and is a member of NAE and the Moles, and a Fellow of the American Consulting Engineers Council.

EDWARD COHEN is managing partner of Ammann & Whitney, Consulting Engineers, and a member of the NAE. He earned a B.S. in Engineering from Columbia University in 1945 and an M.S. in Civil Engineering in 1954. An internationally recognized structural consulting engineer, he has received many awards for his achievements in engineering, including the Illig medal for Applied Science, Columbia University, 1946; Egleston medal Columbia University, 1981, and Goethals medal for Engineering Achievement, Society of American Military Engineers, 1985. His company was responsible for the restoration of the Statue of Liberty and the West Face of the U.S. Capitol.

THOMAS J. EGGUM is the City Engineer for St. Paul, Minnesota. He is responsible for the programs and projects of the Public Works Department of St. Paul. He serves as management peer reviewer and peer review trainer for the American Society of Civil Engineers and Advisory Committee member, self-assessment trainer and local manager for the American Public Works Association's Public Works Management Practices Research Project. He earned a B.C.E. from the University of Minnesota and M.S.C.E. and Master of Public Works Administration from the University of Pittsburgh.

EZRA D. EHRENKRANTZ, FAIA is President, Ehrenkrantz and Eckstut, Architects and holds the Sponsored Chair of Architecture and Building Science at the New Jersey Institute of Technology. An architect and specialist in building systems technology, he was nominated as Construction Man of the Year by ENR magazine and has received the American Institute of Architecture New York Chapter's Medal of Honor. He received his B.A. in architecture from Massachusetts Institute of Technology and M. in architecture from the University of Liverpool.

CARL MONISMITH is Robert Horonjeff Professor of Civil Engineering and Research Engineer at the Institute of Transportation Studies of the University of California at Berkeley. He earned a B.S.C.E. and M.S.C.E. from the University of California at Berkeley. He has served as a consultant to the Asphalt Institute, Chevron Research Corporation, Corps of Engineers, Transport Canada-Air, Woodward Clyde Consultants, Bechtel Corporation, ARE, Inc., and the U.S.A.F., and is a member of the NAE.

ROBERT S. O'NEIL is President of De Leuw, Cather & Company, and President, Parsons Transportation Group. He has been responsible for planning, design, and implementation of major transportation projects, including urban transportation systems, highways, railroads, and other transportation-related facilities, including domestic and international. Mr. O'Neil earned his B.S.C.E. from the University of Notre Dame and his M.C.E. from the Catholic University of America. He is a Fellow of the American Society of Civil Engineers and Institute of Transportation Engineers and a member of several transportation professional societies and the Civil Engineering Research Foundation.

THOMAS D. O'ROURKE, Ph.D., is professor of Civil and Environmental Engineering at Cornell University. He earned a B.S.C.E. from Cornell University, and an M.S.C.E. and Ph.D. from the University of Illinois. He is a member of the NAE, and has received the Collingwood and Huber Research Prizes from the American Society of Civil Engineers for his work on underground facilities, and the C.A. Hogentogler Award from ASTM for his work on the field monitoring of large construction projects. He is a member of several professional societies, including the American Society of Civil Engineers, American Society of Mechanical Engineers, American Society for Testing and Materials, Geotechnical Society, and International Society for Rock Mechanics.

JOSEPH C. PERKOWSKI, Ph.D., is Manager of the Advanced Civil Systems program within the Research and Development Department of Bechtel, responsible for the effective technical and business integration of new technological developments within the strategic plan of Bechtel Civil Inc., the operating arm of Bechtel in the area of civil systems. He was formerly the Staff Programs Manager of the Building Systems

Company, a subsidiary of United Technologies Corporation (1982–1986); Vice President of Oxford Development Group, Ltd. (1979–1982); and Senior Research Officer within the Corporate Department of Environmental and Social Affairs at Petro-Canada. He holds a Ph.D. in Environmental Systems Management from the Department of Civil Engineering at the Massachusetts Institute of Technology.

JOHN RAMAGE is Vice President of CH2M Hill, Inc. His career has included responsibility for major underground and pollution abatement projects. He earned a B.S.C.E. from Washington State University and an M.S.C.E. from the University of Illinois.

SARAH SLAUGHTER, Ph.D., is Assistant Professor of Engineering Management in the Department of Civil Engineering at Lehigh University, involved in conducting research to develop a methodology to evaluate the resource efficiency of existing and emerging technologies. She earned an S.B. in Civil Engineering and Anthropology, S.M. in Technology Policy, and a multidisciplinary Ph.D. in the Management of Technology, Departments of Management and Civil Engineering, from the Massachusetts Institute of Technology. Dr. Slaughter is a member of Signa Xi, National Society of Professional Engineers, the American Society of Civil Engineers, the American Society for Engineering Education, and the New York Academy of Sciences.

JOEL A. TARR, Ph.D., is the Richard S. Caliguiri Professor of Urban and Environmental History and Policy at Carnegie-Mellon University. He is currently working on projects exploring the relationship between industrial wastes and environmental pollution, energy and the environment, and the development of the urban infrastructure. He received his B.S. and M.A. degrees at Rutgers University and his Ph.D. in American History at Northwestern University. He has served as President of the Public History Association.

Staff

ANDREW C. LEMER, Ph.D., an engineer-economist and planner, is the President of the MATRIX Group, Inc. Formerly Division Vice President with PRC Engineering, Inc., he was Director of the Building Research Board from 1988 to 1993. He has served as a consultant to the World Bank, the U.S. Department of Transportation, and the National Institute of Building Sciences. Dr. Lemer is a member of the American Institute of Certified Planners, the American Society of Civil Engineers, the Urban Land Institute, and the American Macro-Engineering Society. He received his S.B., S.M., and Ph.D. degrees in civil engineering from the Massachusetts Institute of Technology, and held a Loeb Fellowship at Harvard University's Graduate School of Design.

RITA B. LEAHY, Ph.D., a National Science Foundation Visiting Scholar and assistant professor (visiting) of civil engineering at Oregon State University, was formerly senior staff engineer with the Strategic Highway Research program. Dr. Leahy received BS and ME degrees in civil engineering at the University of South Carolina and her Ph.D. from the University of Maryland.

MAHADEVAN (DEV) MANI, Ph.D., is the Director of the Division of Infrastructure, Energy, and Environmental Engineering in the National Research Council's (NRC) Commission on Engineering and Technical Systems. The Division encompasses the Energy Engineering, Geotechnical, and Building Research Boards and is engaged in a number of studies for various federal agencies. Dr. Mani came to the NRC in 1989 from TRW.

PETER H. SMEALLIE is a Senior Program Officer in the Division of Infrastructure, Energy, and Environmental Engineering, and formerly Director of the Geotechnical Board. Prior to his work with the NAS-NRC, he was Vice President of Thomas Vonier Associates, an architecture and consulting firm, and was a program director with the American Institute of Architects Research Corporation. He has a degree in Urban Studies from St. Lawrence University.

B

PROSPECTUS

A STUDY OF PHYSICAL INFRASTRUCTURE TECHNOLOGY RESEARCH FOR THE TWENTY-FIRST CENTURY[1]

Building Research Board/Geotechnical Board

(As approved by the Executive Committee of the Governing Board of the National Research Council, May 14, 1991)[2]

PROJECT SUMMARY: The Building Research Board (BRB), in cooperation with the Geotechnical Board, has been asked by the NSF's Division of Mechanical and Structural Systems, Directorate of Engineering, to undertake a study to define the state-of-the-art, basic research needs and priorities related to the technology of physical infrastructure. The study, to be conducted over an 18-month period under the general direction of the National Research Council's (NRC) Committee on Infrastructure (and under the auspices of a strategic program on infrastructure being developed by the Commission on Engineering and Technical Systems (CETS) and spearheaded by the BRB), is an outgrowth of a current project[3] sponsored in part by the NSF; and the NSF is expected to provide funding of $240,000 for this study. The study is planned to incorporate an active outreach program to expand participation beyond the community of the NSF's interests and thereby enhance the study's impact. Partial support of $40,000 for this outreach program will be sought through NRC funds. It is understood that approval of the NSF-supported study does not imply approval of NRC funds for the outreach program. A separate prospectus has been prepared for the outreach program for consideration by the Presidents' Committee at its May 23, 1991 meeting.[4]

ORIGIN AND BACKGROUND: A primary purpose of the NSF's Division of Mechanical and Structural Systems is to expand fundamental engineering knowledge in the broad areas of solid and geomechanics, structures, construction, geomaterials,[5] and building systems engineering, to promote progress in engineering and technology and thereby contribute to national prosperity and security. To this end, the Division has requested that the NRC undertake a study to define the state of the art, basic research needs and priorities in the technology of physical infrastructure. Focused on the fundamental underpinnings of physical infrastructure technology, the study will nevertheless be shaped by the broad national policy debate reflected in a myriad of reports issued in the past decade.[6]

Within this context, this study will undertake to identify key research needs and opportunities for developing and applying new technical knowledge to improve efficiency, effectiveness, and quality of infrastructure facilities and services. It will build upon other research agenda-setting efforts, including work of the BRB and GEOB and the recent Civil Engineering Research Foundation's "National Civil Engineering Research Needs Forum."

A diverse collection of constructed facilities and associated services comprise the physical infrastructure. Despite dependence on many common principles and procedures, each of the major infrastructure "modes" (e.g., bridges or geostructures) is represented by an extensive and specialized body of technical knowledge, professional and managerial people, agencies, institutional relationships, and researchers. This modal diversity inhibits discussion of the cross-cutting issues of infrastructure. Further, serious gaps exist between principal infrastructure technology researchers and state and local government officials and other potential users of this technology.

However, a decade of thinking about infrastructure has suggested to some policy analysts that key problems and opportunities in infrastructure may be better understood by considering the common underlying intellectual body of knowledge, science, and technology of infrastructure. This intellectual body is not well defined, but a number of common features of infrastructure have received study, such as the following examples:

- organic systems of discrete facilities, structures, and users linked together over large areas (e.g., highway or power systems);
- long-lived facilities expected to provide very reliable service under adverse environmental conditions, often critical to basic life safety, public health, and welfare (e.g., water treatment or power generation plants);
- a common set of materials, such as steel, concrete, wood, masonry, and geomaterials used in design and construction;
- extensive use of land, underground space, and aerial, surface, and subsurface connections;

• complex and sometimes unanticipated environmental and social impacts that might be predictable and avoided or mitigated; and

• complex sets of factors that influence what physical service characteristics determine acceptable performance.

Basic research is needed to develop better operational understanding of this common intellectual body of knowledge and to enhance its applications in practice. Such research—in areas such as behavior of soil-cements and network mathematics—will ultimately provide lessons of cross-cutting value for effective infrastructure development and management, leading in turn to enhanced productivity and efficiency in many sectors of the nation's economy. The purpose of the study will be to develop an agenda for this research. This research agenda will present high-priority opportunities the NSF and the research community may use to guide basic infrastructure core research.

PROPOSED ACTIVITY: The study will be conducted under the general direction of the NRC's Committee on Infrastructure and under the auspices of the CETS strategic program on infrastructure being spearheaded by that commission's BRB. Initial activities under the program were approved by the Executive Committee of the NRC's Governing Board in December 1989. The NSF and the U.S. Army Corps of Engineers are among the program's current sponsors.

BRB and the Geotechnical Board will provide staff support and, with other relevant NRC units, consultative assistance for this study. The study will be conducted in three principal stages, with most active work occurring within the middle 8 to 12 months of the anticipated 18-month period:

Stage One. A series of position papers will be prepared to describe the broad meaning and scope of the intellectual body of knowledge of infrastructure and to discuss the national and global significance of this information. Surveys of relatively recent major advances in infrastructure technology, research agenda reports, and new scientific and engineering discoveries (e.g., in construction, geomaterials, building systems, and other fields) that could become the cutting edge of infrastructure technology will establish a baseline for committee deliberations and detailed plans for Stage Two.

Stage Two. Three to four subcommittees will address specific sets of issues in detail. The committee may invite selected experts to participate in this stage of the study, augmenting each subcommittee with two to three such experts. One subcommittee of committee members and staff will integrate all subcommittee materials into a coherent document, and will develop draft committee conclusions and recommendations for committee discussion.

Stage Three. The committee will hold two colloquia (in Washington and Irvine) to review and discuss principal issues identified by the committee. Invited participants in these colloquia will include selected federal, state, and local government representatives and others having interest in and responsibility for infrastructure research and technology policy. Based on discussions at these two colloquia, the committee will finalize its recommendations. The report will be subject to NRC report review procedures.

PRODUCT AND OUTREACH PLAN: Subject to the committee's deliberations and confirmation, the committee's report is anticipated to address (1) the definition of physical infrastructure as a unified concept, the cross-cutting technologies that make the concept meaningful, and the distribution of responsibility for infrastructure technology, performance, and management; (2) the significance of physical infrastructure technology to security and quality of life in the domestic and global economy; (3) the status of modern infrastructure technology, in historic perspective, problems of current technology, and progress on new technology; and (4) a critical review of laboratories, manpower, education programs, and other resources for basic infrastructure technology research.

The committee's report, to be reviewed by members of BRB and the Geotechnical Board, will be subject to NRC's report review procedures.

This study's significance extends well beyond the NSF's usual constituency, encompassing professional engineering communities and state and local government officials. The support and commitment of this broader community will help assure that the study has effective impact. Hence, subject to securing adequate funding, an active outreach program is planned to (1) alert key members of the infrastructure R&D community about the study, (2) engage potential users of infrastructure R&D (e.g., state and local government officials), (3) engage responsible national policy makers, and (4) enhance thereby the likelihood that the committee's work will have real positive impact. Because this program—to be integrated into the study from its outset—exceeds NSF's interests and resources, financial support is being requested from NRC funds.

NOTES

[1]This prospectus became the basis for the agreement between NRC and the NSF, to conduct the study, and was presented to the study committee and discussed at their first meeting.

[2]The "Outreach Program" referred to in this prospectus was subsequently not approved. That portion of the proposed work was deleted from the committee's charge. Subsequent delays in NSF funding led to revisions in the project plan, including substitution of a single workshop for the two that were initially proposed.

[3]Colloquia on Infrastructure for Tomorrow's Metropolis, approved by the Executive Committee of the Governing Board on December 14, 1989.

[4]The outreach plan was not funded and was subsequently deleted from the study.

[5]Geomaterials include man-made textiles, cementitious materials, and metallic components fabricated explicitly for geotechnical applications, as well as soils and rock modified by chemical or physical means to improve their engineering characteristics.

[6]For example, 1984, Joint Economic Committee of the U.S. Congress; 1984, 1987, and 1988, committees of the NRC and National Academy of Engineering; 1988, National Council on Public Works Improvement; and 1990, 1991 (forthcoming), Office of Technology Assessment.

C

WORKSHOP ON INFRASTRUCTURE TECHNOLOGY RESEARCH NEEDS JUNE 2–3, 1993

WORKSHOP PARTICIPANTS

Chairman

JAMES P. GOULD (NAE), Partner, Mueser Rutledge Consulting Engineers, New York, New York

Members

EDWARD COHEN (NAE), Managing Partner, Ammann and Whitney, Consulting Engineers, New York, New York
THOMAS J. EGGUM, Director, Department of Public Works, St. Paul, Minnesota
EZRA D. EHRENKRANTZ, Chair, Architecture and Building Science, School of Architecture, New Jersey Institute of Technology, Newark
CARL MONISMITH (NAE), The Robert Horonjeff Professor of Civil Engineering, University of California at Berkeley
ROBERT S. O'NEIL, President, Parsons Transportation Group, Washington, D.C.
THOMAS D. O'ROURKE (NAE), Professor of Civil Engineering, Cornell University, Ithaca, New York
JOSEPH PERKOWSKI, Manager, Advanced Civil Systems, R&D, Bechtel National Inc., San Francisco, California
JOHN RAMAGE, Vice President, CH2M Hill, Inc., Milwaukee, Wisconsin

SARAH SLAUGHTER, Assistant Professor, Civil Engineering, Lehigh University, Center for Advanced Technology for Large Structural Systems, Bethlehem, Pennsylvania
JOEL TARR, Richard S. Caliguiri Professor of Urban Studies, Carnegie-Mellon University, Pittsburgh, Pennsylvania

Invited Guests

STEVE BARUCH, Manager of Community Initiative, Electric Power Research Institute, Palo Alto, California
ALFONSO CARDENAS, Professor, Department of Computer Science, University of California, Los Angeles
ALBERT A. GRANT, Chairman, Committee on Infrastructure, Consultant, Potomac, Maryland
HILDO HERNANDEZ, Senior Deputy Director, Facilities Operations, Los Angeles County, California
RITA B. LEAHY, Strategic Highway Research Program, National Academy of Sciences, Washington, D.C.
HAROLD MARSHALL, Office of Applied Economics, National Institute of Science and Technology, Gaithersburg, Maryland
ROBERT M. MATYAS, Ithaca, New York
ROBERT PAASWELL, Director of UTRC, Institute for Transportation Systems, City College of New York, New York City
ARTHUR ROSENFELD, Director, Center for Building Science, Lawrence Berkeley Laboratory, Berkeley, California
MASANABU SHINOZUKA, Department of Civil Engineering, Princeton University, New Jersey
PAUL TEICHOLZ, Center for Integrated Facility Engineering (CIFE), Terman Engineering Center, Stanford, California

Staff

ANDREW LEMER, Director, Building Research Board
PETER H. SMEALLIE, Director, Geotechnical Board
MAHADEVAN MANI, Director, Division on Infrastructure, Energy, and Environmental Engineering

D

METHODOLOGY EMPLOYED IN THE STUDY

The committee employed a five-step process in developing its recommended agenda:

1. The committee specified its definition of infrastructure in terms of seven distinct modes or service types: transport, water supply, waste management, energy delivery, telecommunications, institutional buildings, and system-as-a-whole. Within this framework, each committee member proposed a long list of specific questions that research might answer. A review of literature, discussions with representatives of professional organizations, and background materials prepared by staff supplemented committee members' personal knowledge and experience.
2. The staff conducted a cluster analysis of the consolidated list of all committee members' questions. Procedures employed were based on principles of hierarchical decomposition and statistical factor analysis, but the procedures were informally applied. The individual questions were thereby reorganized into broad categories, independently of the seven modal groups within which these questions were proposed. These new categories became the basis for defining niche areas.
3. The committee reviewed and refined the new categories and the initially proposed questions on which the categories were based. Committee members worked in small subcommittees and discussed their work with colleagues outside of the committee. Each subcommittee defined researchable topics and new lists of representative research questions within the emerging three-layered agenda structure (e.g., niche areas, researchable topics, representative research questions).

4. The initial complete draft of the resulting agenda was reviewed and discussed by a wider range of professionals attending a workshop held at the National Academy of Science's Beckman Center in Irvine, California, on July 2 and 3, 1993. During this workshop and in the committee's meeting that followed, the initial draft was revised and expanded. Broad discussions of future infrastructure development provided a background for this work. Implementation strategy and program scope were among the topics discussed by the workshop participants.

5. The committee refined the draft agenda and reconsidered the likely payoffs of research in each topic area. The committee considered how a broad infrastructure program might be structured to address the niche areas, to yield highest possible overall benefits for given levels of research investment. Possible overlaps, conflicts, or mutually beneficial interactions among researchers working on different infrastructure modes on similar research topics were topics considered in this stage of the study. These analyses supported the committee's final recommendations on implementation and staging of the program.

E

SPECIFIC TECHNOLOGIES

The committee and other study participants proposed a number of ideas for new infrastructure technologies, subsystems, and services that warrant exploration. These ideas, for the most part reflecting specific adaptations of technologies used in fields other than infrastructure, might qualify for inclusion in research under several of the committee's recommended major areas of emphasis. However, the committee sought to emphasize a systems approach to infrastructure and research on cross-cutting technologies, and so resolved to de-emphasize such mode-specific topics as those included in this appendix. Nevertheless, the committee recommends that R&D efforts in these areas could yield substantial payoffs as precursors to the next generation of infrastructure technology.

DIGITAL CONTROLS AND "INTELLIGENT" URBAN AREAS

Advances in digital-based control systems have been applied as new products offered by traditional control vendors as well as new systems for the building owner/operator community. Taken together with in-building "tenant services" being offered by facility management professionals, the package of services has been collectively described as the "intelligent building." The concepts of "intelligence" could be extended to entire residential subdivisions, office parks (collections of commercial buildings), or to "new towns" and other large mixed-use developments. Advances in wireless communication applied to intra-building activity (e.g., cellular technology within an office building) as well as within large geographic areas,energy supply and control (e.g., district zoned heating and cooling, photovoltaics), and new control technologies could alter significantly the economics of land use and buildings. Research in these areas could have influence on all infrastructure serving these "intelligent" areas.

PHOTOVOLTAIC ENERGY PRODUCTION

Research to develop commercially viable photovoltaic cells should include consideration of potential applications by small utilities or condominium associations in high-density urban areas. Integrating solar cells with roofing and glass curtainwall elements could yield economic efficiencies that cannot easily be captured by separate development of the energy source and the structures.

PNEUMATIC TUBE TRANSPORT

Pneumatic propulsion systems could be useful as an intra-urban and inter-urban delivery system for small packages (perhaps not exceeding 5 kg) that can fit into easily fabricated tubes. Documents that cannot be telecopied, medical specimens, drugs, factory parts, and consumer goods could be shipped without the uncertainties of weather or the burdens of air pollution. Existing rights-of-way, remote switching, and automated routing could allow such systems to be installed with minimum disruption and wide area coverage.

SUPERCONDUCTIVITY FOR INFRASTRUCTURE APPLICATIONS

Preliminary research results on superconducting materials operating at cryogenic temperatures indicate that substantial benefits can be achieved (e.g., improvements in energy efficiency, applications to new transport systems) if fabrication and operating problems can be solved. Initial applications of the technology are most likely to be in electronics of computers, medical instrumentation, and other small devices. Large-scale applications to infrastructure will pose very different problems, but the substantial benefits warrant research.

AUTOMATED AIRPORT OPERATIONS

Rapid and continuing growth in air transportation demand is outpacing the abilities of existing technology for baggage and cargo handling, people moving, and aircraft ground control and servicing. New technology is needed to match the larger aircraft and advance air-traffic control likely to be introduced in coming decades.